CW00507443

LONDON'S
Sights and Bites

A guide to eating in and around
London's major attractions

Nancy Copeland Ackerman

First published in 2004 by New Holland Publishers (UK) Ltd

London • Cape Town • Sydney • Auckland

Garfield House, 86–88 Edgware Road, London W2 2EA, United Kingdom

www.newhollandpublishers.com

80 Mckenzie Street, Cape Town 8001, South Africa

14 Aquatic Drive, Frenchs Forest, NSW 2086, Australia

218 Lake Road, Northcote, Auckland, New Zealand

10 9 8 7 6 5 4 3 2 1

ISBN 1 84330 569 0

Publishing Manager: Jo Hemmings
Senior Editor: Kate Michell
Copy Editor: Mari Roberts
Assistant Editor: Rose Hudson
Cover Design and Design: Gülen Shevki
Indexer: Dorothy Frame
Production: Joan Woodroffe

Reproduction by Pica Digital Pte Ltd, Singapore
Printed and bound in Malaysia by Times Offset (M) Sdn Bhd

Front cover (clockwise from top left-hand corner): The London Eye; Trafalgar Square;
Harrods' Food Hall; London restaurants; Eating al fresco; Covent Garden.
Spine: Oxo Tower Restaurant, Bar and Brasserie
Back cover (left to right): Theatre Royal, Drury Lane; Along the River Thames; The view
from the National Portrait Gallery's Portrait Restaurant.

Publisher's Note:
Although the author and the publisher have made every effort to ensure that the
information in this book was correct at the time of going to press, they would appreciate
readers' information on any changes that may have occurred in the meantime.

CONTENTS

INTRODUCTION

This book is designed to help visitors to and locals of London find nourishment for the body as well as for the soul and intellect as they explore the city's many wonders. My husband Bob and I have been visiting Great Britain for more than forty years. For the past nine years we have maintained a residence in London. As you can imagine, our family members, friends and acquaintances consider us a reliable source of information about what to see and where to eat in London. This is a heavy burden, but we bear it gladly. In our opinion London is the joy of the Western world, and we want everyone to enjoy this great city and its food as much as we do.

London has so much to see and now has such impressive food that it is impossible to include everything that is interesting and outstanding in a short book such as this. I have, however, included all my time-tested favourites. It is advised that you make a reservation in any restaurant that especially appeals to you. It is also possible that a restaurant described here will close, relocate or undergo a detrimental management change, but I hope not. London is now home to some of the finest, most creative chefs on the planet. If it's been a while since you have visited (and eaten in) this great city, you're in for a delightful surprise. No longer defined by fish 'n' chips with mushy peas (although a great meal in itself), London well deserves its new reputation as the culinary star of Europe. You'll enjoy finding out why.

(£) PRICES AND DINING TIPS

'Budget' – under £5 =
£
'Inexpensive' – under £10 =
££
'Moderate' – under £20 =
£££
'Expensive' – under £35 =
££££
'Very expensive' – over £35 =
£££££

Price categories and symbols are used in the book. Prices are for a meal, including non-alcoholic drink and tip. If you are prepared to pay more for dining in London than in equivalent eateries elsewhere in the UK you will rarely be shocked (and you might occasionally be pleasantly surprised).

In addition, note that every neighbourhood usually has a small café or two where you can get a hearty cooked breakfast (eggs, bacon, grilled tomatoes, mushrooms, toast and tea) for a good deal less than a fiver. And, wonderfully, many of these cafés offer this cooked breakfast all day long. So you can eat well, if inelegantly, for a small amount of money. These cafés are popular with residents and local workers. Pubs are also plentiful and almost always offer snacks and light meals at reasonable prices, although be aware that the quality of the food can vary from frozen ready meals to culinary excellence.

Lunch prices are often cheaper than evening meal prices, so consider making lunch your main meal (you will probably need the fuel, anyway.) Lunch is often a good time to try the more upscale restaurants at friendlier prices. Call to check if they offer reduced prices or special set menus at lunchtime. Many do.

Pre-theatre dining, usually 5.30–7.30pm, often offers set-price menus for wonderful value. This is the same good food that will be ordered later in the evening by others at higher prices. You need to book early and vacate your table by 7.30pm or so.

Fixed-price menus are offered widely, even in the upmarket and famous establishments. This simply means you are getting a smaller selection of two or three courses at lower prices than à la carte.

When you are ordering, the cost of your food – starter, main course and dessert – can seem reasonable. But this price can easily double when you add wine, bottled water and coffee. Minimize these costs by ordering house wine and 'tap' water (at no charge). Also check your bill to see if service has already been included before adding a tip.

➡ LOCATIONS

www.streetmap.co.uk
I originally intended to offer explicit directions to every landmark and restaurant/ café in this book. But the task became so lengthy that I decided simply to tell you the address and the nearest tube station(s). I urge you to pick up a small street map or an *A–Z* to help guide you.

The purpose of this guide is to pinpoint places to eat within a very short walk of a landmark or museum, so you should be able to find most, if not all, places with little effort. The above website is also useful for locating streets if you have access to the Internet.

☎ TELEPHONE CALLS

To make a local phone call within London, use only the last eight digits of the number you are calling. To call London from outside the city, dial the 020 code before the eight-figure number. For example, to call Westminster Abbey to find the times of services, dial 7222 5152 if you are in London, and 020 7222 5152 if you are elsewhere in the country.

🚌 TRANSPORT

www.transportforlondon.gov.uk
Travelling by tube (underground) is the best way to navigate London. Buy a daily travelcard, either off-peak (for use after 9.30am only) or peak (which you can use before 9.30am but costs about a pound extra, depending on the zones

included). If visiting for at least six or seven days, consider getting a weekly travelcard. You will need a passport-sized photo for a weekly (or longer) travelcard, so bring this with you and it will take only a few moments at the ticket office to issue the card. (Most credit cards are accepted for payment.) The convenience (no time restrictions on the weekly card, although the tubes do stop around 12.30am and start again at approximately 5.30am) as well as a reduced price make this worthwhile. Travelcards can be used on all London transport: tubes, buses (show the card to the driver or conductor), Tramlink, DLR (Docklands Light Railway) and National Rail Service within Greater London.

You will be asked which zones you want included. Zones 1 and 2 will enable you to visit *almost* all the entries in this book. Should you wish to travel beyond the central zones, purchase an extension before you begin your journey. You can see the zones on any tube map.

Although tube stations are given for each 'Sight', taking the bus is another good way to get around and also see more of the city 'topside'. Bus guides are easily obtainable, and at the bus stops there are maps showing you where the buses will take you. Be sure to wait for your bus at the correct location, as not all buses stop at all bus stops – the numbers of the buses that do stop are clearly posted on the bus-stop sign.

When you board the bus, show your travelcard. If you are unsure of your destination, the driver or conductor will usually be happy to tell you where to disembark.

Taxis are easily hailed in the main sections of the city, but farther out they can be difficult to find except around train stations. (And they seem to magically disappear when you exit from the theatre at night in the rain; in which case, just head for the closest tube.)

🧒 LONDON WITH CHILDREN

Kids love London. My own children first visited when they were five and seven, and are still making regular visits now with their own children. Just getting around the city is an adventure in itself. My son especially loved riding backwards in the jumpseat of a taxi, as well as climbing up the steep, circular staircase to sit in the top deck of a double-decker bus. Taking the tube or riding the trains from one of the bustling stations all add to the fun.

The places that impressed my children years ago are still here, and still thrill. And today there is even more to entertain and enlighten children, as well as their parents. What amazes me about London is that, with few exceptions, almost every attraction mentioned in this book has some sort of appeal to a young person. History seems to come alive when you see the architecture (the first glimpse of the Tower of London is very exciting) and traipse the halls where others walked hundreds of years ago. Wonderfully, most museums have added programmes to educate and entertain young people. What better gift to give your child?

For up-to-the-minute happenings buy the weekly magazines *What's On* or *Time Out*, both of which have sections for current activities that appeal to youngsters and teenagers. This could include activities in museums (check for days and times) and many extra events during summertime, school holiday breaks and the Christmas season.

✂ EATING OUT WITH CHILDREN

Each museum, gallery or other attraction mentioned in this book welcomes children in their snack bars, cafés and some of the restaurants, and many have special menus for small appetites at reduced cost. For example, the Victoria and Albert Museum offers a Hungry Monkey lunch box (£) of sandwich, fruit, a drink, a biscuit and jelly, while adults have choices of hot dishes, salads, sandwiches, pastries as well as hot and cold drinks, wines and beers.

In general, restaurants and cafés in London do not have facilities other than, perhaps, a special menu that cater to children. Do not automatically expect high chairs, space to park a pram or pushchair, baby-changing facilities or even a warm welcome to the very young (and potentially disruptive) child. That said, I have seen children dining happily with their parents in almost every eating place listed in this book. You know your child and his/her social behaviour, so select the ambience where he or she, and of course you, will be most comfortable. An elegant restaurant probably isn't the place to go with a toddler, whereas an older child might enjoy it tremendously. If you have children who are active and have trouble sitting for the length of time it takes to have a meal, consider the alternative of having a picnic lunch together. Call to enquire in advance about the gardens and special rooms set aside in museums for this purpose. The Pirelli Garden at the Victoria and Albert Museum, for example, is beautiful on a sunny day.

Along the Thames near some of the major attractions, wide pedestrian-only walkways offer space and safety for little ones to run off energy, and there are benches for sitting to enjoy a snack from a nearby kiosk. I love the plaques on these benches that announce 'Everyone needs a place to sit and think'.

As you read the restaurant descriptions you will be able to determine which places are most suitable and welcoming for you and your children. If in doubt, or if you have questions, please phone in advance to ensure a happy occasion for all of you.

ART GALLERIES

To visit the art galleries of London is to experience the cultural heartbeat and history of some of the greatest artists the world has known.
If art is food for the soul, then it is in London that you will find spectacular images on the menu.

The British Museum houses one of the world's finest collections of historical artefacts, from prehistoric times through to the 20th century.

National Gallery

www.nationalgallery.org.uk
Trafalgar Square, London WC2
Tube: Charing Cross, Leicester Square
Telephone: 020 7747 2885
Hours: 10am–6pm (Wednesdays to 9pm); closed 1
January and 24–26 December
Free admission, except for some special exhibitions

Trafalgar Square, with Lord Nelson atop his column and the ubiquitous pigeons, greets you as you emerge from Charing Cross station. This is one of the most photographed areas in the city, so take a moment to admire your surroundings before heading to the National Gallery.

In 1824, the House of Commons agreed to form a new national collection for the enjoyment and education of all, and on this basis entry to the gallery is free, however a donation is appreciated. The gallery is most impressive and needs time to be viewed properly. If time is short hit the highlights, or what you particularly enjoy, then return when you have more time to savour the greatness that lies within. There is almost always a featured presentation going on (for a fee) and, if so, it will be mentioned in *Time Out* and *What's On* magazines.

Permanent collections can be found in these wings:
- Sainsbury Wing: Paintings from 1260 to 1510
- West Wing: Paintings from 1510 to 1600
- North Wing: Paintings from 1600 to 1700

✂ EATING AT THE NATIONAL GALLERY

On the ground floor of the National Gallery's main building the **Gallery Café** (020 7747 2860) serves pastries, fresh sandwiches, soups, hot dishes, desserts and beverages. **£**

Crivelli's Garden in the Sainsbury Wing offers contemporary European cuisine with table service from 11.45am–3pm (later on Wednesdays); book a table on 020 7747 2869. **£££**

Adjoining is the more cosy **Italian Bar**, which is more appealing if you fancy something light. They serve morning and afternoon teas, plus an all-day menu of panini and pizzas. **££**

National Portrait Gallery

www.npg.org.uk
St Martin's Place, WC2
Tube: Charing Cross, Leicester Square
Telephone: 020 7306 0055
Hours: 10am–6pm (Thursday and Friday to 9pm); closed
1 January, Good Friday and 24–26 December
Free admission, except for some special exhibitions

The gallery houses a permanent collection of portraits of well-known men and women from the Middle Ages to the present day. Exhibitions vary and there is always something new to view, with a fee charged for special showings. The galleries are viewer-friendly and you can usually see everything in one visit.

✖ EATING AT THE NATIONAL PORTRAIT GALLERY

On the lower ground floor of the Portrait Gallery is the small, very nice **Portrait Café** with good drinks, a few sandwich selections, light meals and a particularly good coffee and whisky cake that is perfect with a cappuccino. The windows are ceiling

The view from the National Portrait Gallery's Portrait Restaurant

high, exposing the pavement and street above, so you have a mole's eye view of things. Entrance is from the street or through the gift shop. **£**

The **Portrait Restaurant** on the top floor of the Ondaatje Wing offers wonderful views of Trafalgar Square, Whitehall, Westminster Abbey, Big Ben and the London Eye. A talented chef designs modern British dishes, which you can enjoy while gazing out of the window. Book by calling 020 7312 2490. This place is busy and lively, but can be quite smoky. **£££**

The restaurant also has a lounge area with an informal menu and table service (reservations not taken). **££**

Somerset House

www.somerset-house.org.uk
Strand, WC2
Tube: Temple (closed Sundays), Covent Garden, Charing
Cross, Embankment
Telephone: 020 7845 4600
Hours: 10am–6pm; closed 24–26 December; extended
hours apply to the courtyard, river terrace and The
Admiralty restaurant
Free admission to the building, but the individual
collections charge

Somerset House is the home of the Gilbert Collection, the Hermitage Rooms and the Courtauld Institute of Art, and has been at the centre of English history since the 16th century. An extensive restoration has resulted in a magnificent venue for culture, arts and refreshment of body and soul. Allow two to three hours for your visit if you can.

The Gilbert Collection of decorative arts is housed in the Embankment Building. There are frequent new exhibitions as well as stunning permanent displays of European silver, gold snuffboxes and Italian mosaics, a truly world-class collection. For information on guided tours or to book a ticket in advance, call: 020 7420 9410 or email tours@somerset-house.org.uk.

The Hermitage Rooms at Somerset House offer visitors an introduction to Russia's premier museum, the State Hermitage in St Petersburg, one of the four greatest museums of the world, whose enormous collection (3 million objects) can be displayed only five per cent at a time. In Russia it is shown in the Imperial Winter Palace, home of the tsars until the Revolution, in 10 square kilometres of lavishly appointed galleries. For Londoners and London visitors, selections of the collection are regularly shown here in the Hermitage Rooms. The first exhibition featured the treasures of Catherine the Great, Empress of Russia 1762–96: her personal possessions, her gifts to family members and her many lovers, as well as diplomatic gifts. On view were paintings, medals, jewels, boxes, weapons (including an exquisite miniature set of swords created for her grandson) and many other works of art. On the heels of this enormously successful first exhibition came 'French Drawings and Paintings from the Hermitage: Poussin to Picasso'. Exhibits are constantly rotated. Tickets are sold for timed slots to ensure there is no crowding and can be obtained on the spot or by calling 020 7413 3398 (24 hours) in advance.

The small Courtauld Institute of Art – you can see everything in one visit – houses world-famous paintings such as Edouard Manet's (1832–83) 'Bar at the Folies-Bergère' and Renoir's 'La Loge', which you can absorb from one of the thoughtfully provided and carefully placed benches or chairs. The finest collection of Impressionist paintings in Britain is here, as well as masterpieces by Botticelli – all in the most beautiful 18th-century buildings in London. Hours are Monday–Saturday 10am–6pm, with last entrance at 5.15pm; Sundays and bank holidays 12 noon–6pm. The telephone number is 020 7848 2526. Admission is free to all on Mondays from 10am–2pm.

A special place to take a break in the fresh air is outdoors at Somerset House in the Edmond J. Safra Court, a summer venue for open-air events. There are tables, chairs and umbrellas and children and the young at heart will enjoy cooling off in the choreographed dancing fountains, which bubble and rise unpredictably. Of course you will get wet! Sitting in this area gives you the inside view (that cannot be seen from the street) of the very beautiful buildings of Somerset House and the Courtauld Institute of Art. This is a refreshing and peaceful oasis to enjoy and, being just off the busy Strand, is a good place to know about. In winter, an ice-skating rink replaces the dancing fountains. It is picture-postcard pretty, and a wonderful stop if you are visiting London with children during the cold season.

✂ EATING AT SOMERSET HOUSE

The Admiralty (020 7845 4646), the lofty, elegant dining rooms in gorgeous Somerset House, is the perfect setting for the top-flight French cuisine found here. Three rooms offer up-market indoor dining, and an outside terrace covered with an awning is open in fine weather for views of the Thames and the South Bank. The food is simple, modern French with an emphasis on fish dishes. It is elegant but not cheap. Unusually, they have a delightful vegetarian menu, too. **££££**

The **River Terrace Café** has seating outdoors. It is also on the expensive side but offers fine views of the Thames, Big Ben, the London Eye and the river traffic flowing by. **££££**

There is also the **Introductory Gallery Café**

The dancing fountains in the courtyard of Somerset House

and the **Deli**, which both serve light meals, hot and cold drinks, sandwiches, salads, yogurts and pastries. We bought our afternoon coffee and cake, took it outside on the terrace and enjoyed the same view as the diners in the River Terrace Café for a lot less money. Chairs and small tables make for a comfortable spot to rest your feet, let your children move about safely and take in the glorious view while enjoying some refreshment. **£**

There is also a café in the Courtauld Institute of Art. **££**

✕ The George

213 The Strand, WC2
Tube: Temple
Telephone: 020 7427 0941

This popular pub, built in 1723, is a favourite of the local barristers from the Royal Courts of Justice and their clients. The setting remains as it was in the days when it was patronized by the likes of writer Samuel Johnson (1709–84) and novelist Oliver Goldsmith (1728–74), who were regulars enjoying their draughts of beer.

The fare is bangers and mash, fish and chips, steak and kidney pie and the like, and you'll enjoy the original architecture and, perhaps, the ghost of the headless cavalier who haunts the basement dining area. **££**

✕ Simpson's in the Strand

www.simpsons-in-the-strand.co.uk
100 The Strand, WC2
Tube: Charing Cross
Telephone: 020 7836 9112

Simpson's is expensive, and you need to be smart-casual at least (jacket and tie for men in the main dining room; and no jeans or trainers anywhere) and the waiters can be snooty. They will always ask if you've booked and be quite put out if you have not. If you can get past that, this is a restaurant to try at least once just for the experience.

Open since 1828, the Victorian interior has Adam panelling, crystal, formal waiters and a tail-coated carver who expertly slices your roasted meat – sirloin of beef, saddle of mutton with redcurrant jelly, Aylesbury duckling and so on – from a silver trolley at your table. If you go only once, have roast beef with Yorkshire pudding and finish with the treacle tart or Stilton and a small glass of port.

They also serve a huge breakfast that will take years off your life – sausage, fried eggs, two kinds of bacon, black pudding, lamb's kidneys, potatoes and cabbage, baked beans, lamb's liver, fried bread, mushrooms and tomatoes. It is a veritable heart attack on a plate.

A pre-theatre dinner is served for a reasonable set price. **£££–££££**

Tate Britain

www.tate.org.uk
Millbank, SW1
Tube: Pimlico
Telephone: 020 7887 8000
Hours: 10am–6pm; closed 24–26 December
Free admission, except for some special exhibitions

Located near Vauxhall Bridge fronting the Thames, this is where you will see the national collection of British paintings from 1400 to the present day, and the national collection of 20th-century paintings and sculpture. The English painter J.M.W. Turner left to the nation, upon his death in 1851, his paintings, watercolours and sketchbooks, which are housed in the Clore Gallery. He wanted his finished works, some hundred paintings, displayed together underneath one roof. In addition, his personal collection of 19,000 watercolours and 300 paintings can also be seen. Turner lived and died in Chelsea on the banks of the Thames, a couple of miles upriver.

Tate Britain's new galleries also hold a permanent collection of paintings by Blake, Reynolds, Gainsborough, Hogarth and Constable, as well as several Pre-Raphaelite beauties. Tate Britain houses British art exclusively. The new Tate Modern at Southwark holds the modern art collection.

On Sundays from 12 noon to 5pm and often on school holidays, children aged three to 12 can enjoy the Art Trolley activities: drawing, collage, games and puzzles and making things. Artspace is a comfortable family area off the main galleries with hands-on sculpture activities, jigsaws, constructions, games and books. And there are many more activities for children. To find out more or to book for special events, call Tate Ticketing at 020 7887 3959.

✕ EATING AT TATE BRITAIN

The internationally renowned **Tate Britain Restaurant** (situated on the lower level) has a famously inventive menu; reservations are strongly advised (020 7887 8825). Wonderful food and murals by Whistler are a terrific combination. **£££–££££**

Opposite the restaurant is the self-service **Tate Café & Espresso Bar**. Hot dishes include pasta and pies and there are ciabattas with grilled vegetables; mozzarella, spinach and tomato; beef and horseradish. There are plenty of choices of drinks and cakes. Children enjoy making their own food selections here. **£–££**

Tate Modern

www.tate.org.uk
Bankside, SE1
Tube: Blackfriars, Southwark
Telephone: 020 7887 8000
Hours: 10am–6pm Sunday–Thursday; 10am–10pm Friday and Saturday
Free admission, except for some special exhibitions

Architects Herzog & de Meuron creatively redeveloped Bankside Power Station into this fabulous gallery on the south bank of the Thames, opposite St Paul's Cathedral. The celebrated design and its sheer scope have already made it the biggest free attraction in London. Natural light floods the gallery spaces and many sculptures are sited in unusual places. Its displays of international modern art include works by Bacon, Dalí, Picasso, Matisse, Rothko and Warhol. The exciting building will thrill you as much as the art inside.

Tate Modern has an extremely creative programme for children called Artmixx. Expect lively journeys around the gallery, Tate Tales (where poets and storytellers introduce displays through stories and word games) and the Time Capsule history trail. Most activities are for ages five and up, but some are suitable for three-year-olds. To find out what is currently on and to reserve a place, call 020 7887 8888.

✕ EATING AT TATE MODERN

The **Café on level 7** (020 7401 5020) is made outstanding by its excellent views of central London, including St Paul's Cathedral. With just a glass pane between you and the Thames, it's a terrific venue for your gallery break, and also great just for coffee or a snack if you don't have a lot of time. The brasserie-style food is very good, probably because the consultant to this eatery and the **Café on level 2** is Jeremy King, founder of Le Caprice and The Ivy (see page 136) restaurants. This is a double-whammy celebration of culture and cuisine. It is open for dinner (until 9.30pm) Friday and Saturday only. No booking, no smoking. **££**

The **Café on level 2** has the same menu as the **Café on level 7**, but you should opt for the more lofty view upstairs. The menus change seasonally, so you are assured of the freshest and best. **££**

Snacks are also available from the **Kiosk** at the North Entrance and the **Espresso Bar** on level 4. **£**

The Tate Modern is housed in a converted power station

The Wallace Collection

www.wallacecollection.org
Hertford House, Manchester Square, W1
Tube: Bond Street, Baker Street
Telephone: 020 7563 9500
Hours: 10am–5pm Monday–Saturday; 12 noon–5pm
Sunday; closed 24–26 December, January 1, Good Friday
and May Day Bank Holiday
Free admission

This delightful small gallery in a late-18th-century townhouse is not exactly a secret, but it does seem to be visited more by Londoners than by tourists. It is tucked away on Manchester Square just a short walk from Bond Street tube station. On view are exquisite selections of 17th- and 18th-century paintings, china, furniture, arms and armour, miniatures and virtu, and a visit here can even be combined with your shopping trip to Oxford Street. The gift shop has nice postcards and stationery.

✕ EATING AT THE WALLACE COLLECTION

The **Café Bagatelle** is a relatively new addition to the museum, located in the Sculpture Garden in a bright conservatory setting. It is very popular and reservations are almost always necessary for the busy lunchtimes: call 020 7563 9505. **£££**

✕ ST CHRISTOPHER'S PLACE

Not far from the museum, hidden down an alley going north from busy Oxford Street but approachable from several directions, is St Christopher's Place. Leaving The Wallace Collection walk back towards Oxford Street on Duke Street, turning left onto Barrett Street – St Christopher's Place is on your left. You can also enter from Oxford Street via an alley or James Street. Once in the square you will be rewarded with some lovely shops and good dining choices.

✕ Carluccio's Caffé

www.carluccios.com
St Christopher's Place, W1
Tube: Bond Street
Telephone: 020 7935 5927

This café, one of several (their first and premier restaurant is in Covent Garden), offers a deli that is all Italian with meats, cheeses, oils, vinegars and olives, along with coffees, sandwiches and other delicious treats for taking out or eating in the informal dining area (possibly sharing a table). In nice weather outdoor dining is an option.

Carluccio's is owned by Antonio Carluccio, who has written several cookery books, which feature, among many Italian classics, his speciality: mushrooms. **££**

✕ Apostrophe

www.apostropheuk.com
23 Barrett Street, W1
Tube: Bond Street
Telephone: 020 7355 1001

This is a new location for this delicious French café, which has, bar none, the best hot chocolate in London. The café's menu items and the bakery's breads and pastries on display are for eating in or taking out.

As well as a few counter stools and outside tables, you can eat downstairs in a slick, almost Art Deco-style dining area, which is comfortable and friendly.

Open from 8am on weekdays and 9am on weekends, you can begin your day here with a filling breakfast, including a pastry from the dozen or so on offer, and of course the thick hot chocolate. The chocolate can also come 'spiced', which adds an exotic flavour. Coffees, teas, cold drinks and fresh organic fruit juices are also available. Fine for children, inside or out. **£–££**

✕ Bean Juice

St Christopher's Place, W1
Tube: Bond Street
Telephone: 020 7724 3840

If you have children with you they will be happy with the flavours of milkshake (Oreo chocolate, vanilla, fresh banana and peanut butter, strawberry) and ice-cream floats (root beer, blue bubble gum, green apple and more), and perhaps even the good-for-you smoothies, too. A large variety of juice cocktails is also available.

The food department is not huge, but offers artisan-bread sandwiches, bagels, salads and fresh soup, all made fresh each morning in the downstairs gallery. Tables and chairs in the back. **£–££**

HISTORICAL LONDON

London's vibrant history is alive and well, and the imprint of 2,000 years of turbulence and triumph greet you at every turn. The city is a treasure trove of magnificent museums, stunning architecture, royal pomp and pageantry and, of course, there is always a chance to sample traditional British fare.

The Houses of Parliament are a Victorian masterpiece whose intricate architectural detailing never ceases to astound.

Buckingham Palace

Web: www.the-royal-collection.org.uk
Tube: Green Park, St James's Park, Victoria
Telephone: 020 7321 2233
Hours: 9.30am–5pm, 1 August–28 September
Admission charge

The Changing of the Guard takes place every other day at 11.30am. Since the dates change from odd to even on a regular basis, you will have to check for the times at the Visitorcall line: 09064 123411. There is no guard change in very wet weather, and times may alter on days when state events take place. However, you can view Buckingham Palace from the outside at any time, as well as see the Victoria Memorial that faces the gate. When the queen is in residence the Royal Standard (flag) will be flying and you might even catch sight of her coming or going.

During August and September (only), Buckingham Palace is open to the public. If you are visiting London during these months, make this a top-of-the-list destination. The elaborate rooms and the art and furniture collections are stunning, and the paintings are, of course, of museum quality. Unfortunately, there is no sense of the domestic life of the queen, and some of the interiors are opulent kitsch, but still… you are walking on the same floors as royalty past and present.

■ QUEEN'S GALLERY

www.royal.gov.uk
Buckingham Palace,
Buckingham Palace Road, SW1
Tube: Victoria
Telephone: 020 7321 2233
Hours: 10am–5.30pm
Admission charge

Freshly refurbished in time for the queen's jubilee in 2002, the Queen's Gallery holds one of the world's greatest art collections – representing five centuries of royal artistic passion and taste. The sculpture *Fountain Nymph* by Antonio Canova is worth the visit alone. Also on view, in addition to majestic oils, exquisite pen and ink drawings and two of the finest porcelain services ever made by the Worcester and Rockingham factories, is the queen's shimmering Diamond Diadem, *c.* 1820, the tiara she wears on coins and stamps.

◼ ROYAL MEWS

www.royal.gov.uk
Buckingham Palace,
Buckingham Palace Road, SW1
Tube: Victoria
Telephone: 020 7321 2233
Hours: 11am–4pm, 1 March to
31 October; 10am–5pm, August
and September
Admission charge

The queen's horses and
the carriages used on state

occasions, including the
extremely ornate Coronation
Coach, which was built in
1761, are on public display
at the Royal Mews.

✕ Bumbles

16 Buckingham Palace Road, SW1
Tube: Victoria
Telephone: 020 7828 2903

This is traditional British food

in an old, well-established, bistro-type restaurant. The atmosphere is 'olde worlde' and charming. Closed on Sundays; reservations recommended. **££–£££**

✕ Noodle Noodle

www.noodle-noodle.co.uk
18 Buckingham Palace Road, SW1
Tube: Victoria
Telephone: 020 7931 9911

Very *very* good noodle and rice dishes served in a pleasant atmosphere of stripped wooden floors, pale colours and lighted niches holding Chinese artefacts. It's a good choice for a quick and delicious meal. Restaurant manager Annie Wong makes sure the kitchen and service is always top-notch. Note: the step up into the restaurant is steep. **£–££**

At Buckingham Palace the Royal Standard is only raised when the Queen is in residence

✂ Tiles

36 Buckingham Palace Road, SW1
Tube: Victoria
Telephone: 020 7834 7761

All main courses here come with a glass of house wine. Almost half the items on the menu are vegetarian and there are also daily specials on the blackboard and a snack menu that includes platters to share. **££–£££**

✂ City Harvest

38 Buckingham Palace Road, SW1
Tube: Victoria
Telephone: 020 7630 9781

Although they offer good hot breakfasts and lunches, their real strength is in the sandwiches, both 'regular' and 'gourmet', which makes choosing agonizing. They can make up a take-away package for you to enjoy at home or in your hotel if you have reached a stage in your sightseeing day where you want to take a break and relax but still eat well. **££**

✂ Balls Bros

www.ballsbrothers.co.uk
50 Buckingham Palace Road, SW1
Tube: Victoria
Telephone: 0870 243 9759

There are several Balls Bros pub-bistros around town and all are good. They offer good food and drink all day with 'between the bread' selections, hot main dishes and a good listing of bites. A nice stop when you want a light meal. Children are discouraged as the clientèle is mainly business people. **££**

Kensington Palace

www.hrp.org.uk
Kensington Gardens, W8
Tube: Queensway, High Street Kensington (south side), Notting Hill Gate
Telephone: 0870 751 5170
Hours: 10am–6pm, 1 March to 31 October; 10am–5pm, 1 November to end February
Admission charge

The former home of Diana, Princess of Wales and princes William and Harry, Kensington Palace sits in beautiful Kensington Gardens and offers daily tours. It was here, in 1837, that Victoria was awakened with the news that her uncle, William IV, had died and that she was now Queen of England. Kensington Palace was also home to the late Princess Margaret.

State apartments include furniture, ceiling paintings and Victorian rooms. Exhibited throughout are works of art from the Royal Collection and the Royal Ceremonial Dress Collection. The ground-floor gift shop sells Princess Diana mementos. Since Diana's death, a memorial park for children has been built nearby, Peter Pan Park, and if you have a child with you (no admission without one) do visit. Kensington Gardens and the beautiful grounds are open daily to the public (see page 101). Here you can see the Round Pond and the imposing Albert Memorial. It is a testament to Victorian taste – and quite amazing.

✕ EATING IN KENSINGTON GARDENS

The Orangery, open 10am–5pm, is in a conservatory built in 1704 by Queen Anne for her tea parties. It has been converted into a lovely restaurant featuring Corinthian columns, statuary brought from Windsor Castle by the royal family, a soaring ceiling and a pair of Grinling Gibbons' wood carvings. The floor-to-ceiling windows look out upon the palace and gardens, and the view is glorious.

Breakfast, served between 10am and 12 noon, features butter croissants and Chelsea buns, plus hot chocolate, teas and coffees. You can also enjoy teas – both morning and afternoon – and lovely luncheons. The desserts are displayed as you enter, so it's easy to decide whether you'll save room for something luscious to end your meal (lemon tart, the queen's cake and the coffee walnut cakes are all good). **££**

✕ Diana's Café
Bayswater Road
Tube: Notting Hill Gate

The owner of this small café has filled the walls with photos of the late princess, including one of himself with Diana. She was touched by his admiration and could occasionally be seen having coffee here. The usual café food is offered plus many Greek dishes and pastries. **£**

✕ Le Piaf

19–21 Notting Hill Gate, W11
Tube: Notting Hill Gate
Telephone: 020 7727 8810

This pleasant French bistro specializes in casual dining, fresh ingredients and changing daily specials (there is always a meat, poultry and vegetarian selection). Open for morning coffee and pastries plus full English breakfast, then throughout the day for full meals and snacks. Full bar available. ££

St Martin-in-the-Fields Church

www.stmartin-in-the-fields.org
Trafalgar Square, WC2
Tube: Charing Cross, Leicester Square
Telephone: 020 7766 1100
Hours: All day, evenings vary according to concerts and services
Free admission, except for evening concerts

The present church is a fine example of Baroque architecture featuring an elegant spire and portico, and was designed by architect James Gibbs and completed in 1726. It replaced a royal parish church that had been built for Henry VIII in 1544, but there are records of a church being on this site since Norman times.

Some of the most wonderful musical events in town take place here. Their free lunchtime concerts at 1pm each Monday, Tuesday and Friday feature an extraordinarily wide range of performers and repertoire from all over the world. The evening concerts by candlelight, with tickets at very reasonable prices, feature string ensembles, violin concertos, choral and chamber music, Bach, Mozart, Vivaldi, Handel and more. Do try and attend one of these, as it is a magical experience. The church has a musical history, too, as Handel once played the church's first organ and Mozart is reputed to have given a concert here.

In the basement there is a bookshop and a brass-rubbing centre where you can re-create romantic ladies and knights in armour from the age of chivalry. The staff will gladly assist you in getting started, and the result is a special souvenir. There is a small charge for the brass-rubbing.

✂ EATING AT ST MARTIN-IN-THE-FIELDS

The **Café in the Crypt** (020 7839 4342) is always fun to visit. Its opening hours also make it convenient for a pre-theatre supper. Enter down the stairs from Duncannon Street. The cafeteria-style restaurant will be to your right. If you look down you will see that you are walking over ancient burial crypts, but don't let that put you off your food.

Take a moment to read the blackboard and glance at the offerings for the day, as you will surely put too much on your tray if you don't decide ahead of time.

Expect beautiful salads, homemade soup and rustic breads, or perhaps go for a blow-out nosh with duck glazed with cranberry chutney followed by apple crumble with lashings of cream or an incredible crème brûlée – all prepared by their in-house chefs.

From Thursday to Saturday there are often live jazz performances in the evening. **£–££**

✂ **For other dining options near St Martin-in-the-Fields Church, please see the listings for Covent Garden on pages 46–51 .**

Houses of Parliament
www.parliament.uk
Westminster, SW1
Tube: Westminster
Telephone: 0870 906 3773 for Summer Opening times
Hours: UK residents can visit on Monday mornings and Friday afternoons with their local MP. Overseas visitors can visit Monday to Saturdays during the afternoon throughout the Summer Opening (July–October)
Admission charge for Summer Opening

The interior is not open to the public but it is possible to attend the debates when the House is in session (always call first to confirm exact times and ticket details). Gain access by joining the line at St Stephen's entrance.

The Houses of Parliament are the stronghold of Britain's democracy. The House of Commons and the House of Lords are in the former royal Palace of Westminster where the king resided until Henry VIII moved to Whitehall. The earlier buildings (founded in the 11th century, rebuilt in the 13th and 14th century) were destroyed by fire in 1834, and the current majestic Gothic Revival buildings were erected in 1840. There are more than a thousand rooms and two miles of corridors within. The very familiar clock tower at the eastern end houses Big Ben, the largest bell in the chime, which weighs almost 14 tons. At night a light shines from the tower when Parliament is in session.

✗ **Please see the list of local restaurants and cafés on pages 32–33.**

10 Downing Street, home of
Britain's Prime Minister

Downing Street

www.number-10.gov.uk
10 Downing Street, SW1
Tube: Westminster
No admission

Since 1732, when it was acquired by Sir Robert Walpole, 10 Downing Street has been the official residence of Britain's prime ministers. Downing Street is a short, one-block street that runs between the top of St James's Park (Horse Guards Road) and Whitehall, and is opposite the Foreign Office. Since the events of 11 September 2001 in New York, extreme security measures have been put in place, and you can only get a glimpse of this rather modest house from the top of the street. The Chancellor of the Exchequer's residence is next door, at No. 11.

 **Please see the list of local restaurants and cafés on pages 32–33.**

Westminster Abbey

www.westminster-abbey.org
Parliament Square, SW1
Tube: Westminster
Telephone: 020 7222 5152 (for times of services)
Hours: 9.30am–4.45pm Monday–Friday (6–7.45pm on Wednesdays); 9.30am–2.45pm Saturday
Admission charge

This beautiful Gothic building, with its instantly recognizable square twin towers, is both the shrine and symbol of what this ancient country has stood for and still stands for. This is where royalty is crowned and where many lie buried. Its history dates back to 1065 when Edward the Confessor founded a Benedictine abbey on this spot and it now overlooks Parliament Square. Be sure to see Poets' Corner, Statesman's Aisle, the coronation chair and the wondrous fan-vaulted ceiling of the Henry VII chapel. Always a popular tourist attraction, its attendance has increased 300 per cent since millions of people around the world saw the funeral of Diana, Princess of Wales. Such an increase has resulted in a more restricted viewing of some areas. The tour conducted by a resident clergyman is highly recommended and worth the extra charge. Book at the abbey inquiry desk or call 020 7222 7110. Note: There are no public toilets in the abbey; public conveniences are situated in the small park opposite.

Inside the Abbey is a small **snack bar** serving coffee, tea, cold drinks and light snacks, while in fine weather, outside kiosks offer ice creams. **£**

✕ Cinnamon Club

www.cinnamonclub.com
The Old Westminster Library,
Great Smith Street, SW1
Tube: Westminster, St James's Park
Telephone: 020 7222 2555

Just one block from Westminster Abbey and the Houses of Parliament, and located in the Old Westminster Library, this restaurant and bar is a terrific meal option in an area of sparse choices. The menu is sophisticated Indian. There are many vegetarian choices, too.

The dining room of this private members' club is open to the public, and the outstanding food is prepared by an inspired chef, Vivek Singh. The club's members, however, have the luxury of savouring their food with an after-dinner cigar or brandy in the cigar room.

Guest chefs ensure that the menu is always fresh and exciting. **£££–££££**

✕ Pickles

6 Old Queen Street, SW1
Tube: Westminster
Telephone: 020 7222 8749

Just down an alley is this small, but great, sandwich bar. Just the spot if you want to eat and run, but still have a delicious sandwich. Everything is fresh, and the staff, including Nasser the owner, will custom-make your sandwich just as you like it. **£**

✕ Wesley's Café

Central Hall, Westminster, SW1
Tube: Westminster

Walk past Dean's Yard and cross the street onto Storey's Gate then walk a few steps to Central Hall. Wesley's Café faces the park square and the Queen Elizabeth Conference Centre. Follow the signs downstairs to the cafeteria for hot soups and main courses (such as tuna steak) with fresh vegetables and wonderful sweets (and waffles). Sandwiches and salads are good value. Cream teas are served 3–6pm in the bright conservatory – often with piano music. This is a modest place and family friendly. **£**

St Paul's Cathedral

www.stpauls.co.uk
Tube: St Paul's
Telephone: 020 7236 4128
Hours: 8.30am–4pm Monday–Saturday
Admission charge for adults, children go free

This beautiful cathedral, built by Sir Christopher Wren between 1675 and 1710, is the architectural genius's ultimate masterpiece. Inside you will see ironwork by Jean Tijou and carvings by Grinling Gibbons. View the ceiling mosaics and Sir James Thornhill's dome paintings; climb into the Whispering Gallery (259 steps) for its special effects, then ascend to the top of the golden dome (another 218 steps) for a spectacular 360-degree view of London. Be warned that the last 153 steps are difficult. Entombed here are Lord Nelson, the Duke of Wellington and Sir Christopher Wren himself. Half the world saw the interior when Prince Charles and Lady Diana married here in 1981. St Paul's stands on the site of two previous cathedrals dating back to 604 AD. There is no admission charge for Sunday worship or other services of matins, Holy Communion and evensong.

✂ EATING AT ST PAUL'S CATHEDRAL

Underneath the cathedral is the wonderful, atmospheric, small **Crypt Café** (020 7246 8358), which has tables scattered beneath the high stone arches. The menu is not huge but changes daily, features what is market fresh and always has a selection of hot dishes and soups as well as delicious sandwiches and pastries. The spaciousness of the eating area makes this a pleasant stop if you have children with you. **£–££**

Next to the café is the larger, well-appointed **Refectory Restaurant** catered by Milburn's, whose high standards are enjoyed in many museums and cathedrals in the UK. Here you can have an elegant meal with wine and starters, or a reasonably priced hot filled baguette with a bowl of soup (a vegetarian option is also available). Lunch is served 11am–3.30pm, and 3–5pm there is a tea-time menu with refectory tea (sandwiches and scones) and cathedral high tea (cheese rarebit with cakes) on offer. **£–££**

■ MILLENNIUM BRIDGE

River Thames, between St Paul's and Tate Modern
Tube: St Paul's
Hours: All day, every day
Free admission

This futuristic bridge links the Tate Modern on the south bank of the Thames with St Paul's Cathedral on the north side. The bridge got off to a shaky start when pedestrians got 'seasick' when crossing it due to excess wobbling. The bridge has since been stabilized and reopened to foot traffic. Walking across the Thames is exciting, and when you head from south to north there is a wonderful vista of St Paul's.

■ ST BRIDE'S CHURCH

www.stbrides.com
Fleet Street, EC4
Tube: Blackfriars
Telephone: 020 7427 0133
Hours: 9am–4.45pm
Free admission

Mr Rich, an 18th-century local baker, designed the wedding cake style of graduated tiers after viewing the spires of St Bride's and earned a fortune making cakes resembling the shape of the steeple. The crypt below the church preserves some Roman ruins and has information on the site's history which, spanning nearly 2,000 years, is fascinating. There is a lovely garden with benches beside the church.

✕ Ye Olde Cheshire Cheese

145 Fleet Street, EC4
Tube: St Paul's, Blackfriars
Telephone: 020 7353 6170

History abounds in this tucked-away pub which was rebuilt in 1667 (the foundation stone was laid in the 13th century). The writer Samuel Johnson's (1709–84) house is located on the next block and is worth seeing. The pub's food is good and is served in a storybook atmosphere.

The Baroque architecture of St Paul's Cathedral

Always on the menu is Ye Famous Pudding (filled with steak, kidney, mushrooms and game) and Scottish roast beef with Yorkshire pudding, plus grilled chops, steak and kidney pie and so on. It's also good for an afternoon beer and snack stop, for those who prefer not to brave the meal-time crowds. The pub's history and ambience make this such a popular spot that I would advise you either to arrive early for lunch (before any tour groups arrive) or make sure to book a table in advance. It would be a shame to miss this wonderful place. **££–£££**

The original Globe burnt down in 1613 but has now been rebuilt to house the Shakespeare Globe Trust, an educational charity dedicated to the experience and international understanding of Shakespeare in performance. The theatre season runs from May to September with 600 cheap tickets available for every performance. For tickets call 020 7401 9919. Beneath the theatre in the Underglobe is a permanent collection of exhibits telling the story of actor-director Sam

Shakespeare's Globe in Southwark is a superb
reconstruction of a 16th-century theatre

Wanamaker's determined campaign to rebuild the Globe as authentically as possible. The exhibition also provides insight into the work that is undertaken both on and off stage. As it says in their brochure, 'A visit to Shakespeare's Globe may change the way you think about Shakespeare.'

✕ EATING AT SHAKESPEARE'S GLOBE

Enjoy a panoramic view of the Thames and St Paul's Cathedral along with your meal in the **Shakespeare's Globe Café**, open 10am–6pm (telephone 020 7902 1576). During theatre season the café is open until 15 minutes after the performance. The morning menu features delights such as plum upsidedown cake and sticky orange marmalade flapjacks, as well as croissants. At lunchtime there are sandwich choices, as well as main dishes such as ginger, mustard and Madeira-glazed chicken or a pasta of the day with green leaf salad. **£–££**

Or try the **Shakespeare's Globe Restaurant** (telephone 020 7928 9444) where up-market modern British fare is served. Light dishes are available, as well as more hearty fare. Open for lunch 12 noon–2.30pm and for supper 5.30–10pm. During the theatre season, May to September, last orders are taken at 11pm. You could give yourself a very elegant evening of Shakespeare and fine dining here. Reservations are recommended. **££–£££**.

There is also a **coffee shop** in the main foyer, which serves drinks and snacks. **£**

The Tower of London
www.hrp.org.uk
Tower Hill, EC3
Tube: Tower Hill
Telephone: 0870 756 6060
Hours: 9am–6pm Monday–Saturday and 10am–6pm Sunday, March–October; 9am–5pm Tuesday–Saturday and 10am–5pm Sunday–Monday, November–February; closed 24–26 December & 1 January
Admission charge

This is where you will find the famous Beefeaters who guard the Tower and who will graciously allow themselves to be photographed with you (sign up for one of their guided tours). The Tower spans over a thousand years of history and has been used as a palace, prison and execution site. You can see the Crown Jewels, Traitor's Gate, the Royal Armouries and the famous black ravens who have never left the area in all its history. There is a costumed re-enactment of daily life as it was hundreds of years ago. The Tower remains spooky to this day – clanking chains, headless bodies, phantom soldiers and icy blasts give a shivery atmosphere of impending doom. Children love this place.

The Tower is divided into several structures: the White Tower built in 1078, the Bloody Tower where Sir Walter Raleigh spent 13 years before being executed, the Beauchamp Tower, Traitors' Gate and Tower Green where two wives of Henry VIII, Anne Boleyn and Catherine Howard, lost their lives to the executioner's axe. Plan to spend a considerable amount of time here in order to see everything. It is wonderful.

Very good meal choices are close by, but you'll need some directions as no street passes directly within this area.

When you exit the Tower Hill tube station go down the stairs outside and take the footpath to the left (the right takes you to the Tower of London entrance). Follow the footpath under the overhead bridge to the St Katherine's Dock area. This will be signposted. You will pass a **Riverside Restaurant** (cafeteria style, pleasant but plain interior) and the **Tower Patisserie** (small café offering just pastries and coffees). Straight on you will see the Dickens Inn and will reach it after crossing a small footbridge. This is a charming short walk past sailboats moored in the cove.

✕ EATING AT THE TOWER OF LONDON

Within the tower's walls you will find the **New Armouries** restaurant. Here, you can get everything from a simple coffee and cake to a hot meal. As is often the case with restaurants attached to tourist sights, this is quite expensive for what you get, but it is an easy pitstop if you have children with you. **££**.

Drinks and snacks are also available from the **Tower Café** and **Kiosk** found on the wharf.

✕ Dickens Inn

St Katherine's Way, E1
Tube: Tower Hill
Telephone: 020 7488 2208

This is an 1830s brick warehouse on three floors that now houses several places to eat. Large windows afford a sweeping view of the Thames and Tower Bridge. On the ground level are a bar and the Tavern Room (11am–11pm) serving soup, sandwiches, lasagne, chilli and snacks for children. **£.**

On the floor above is Pizza on the Dock (12 noon–10pm) with four sizes of pizza that are good for children, plus some tasty soups, pasta and salads. **££.**

On the top floor is the **Dickens Restaurant** (12 noon–3pm and 6.30–10pm), which serves modern British fare. **££–£££**

✕ Blueprint Café

www.conran.com
Design Museum,
28 Shad Thames, SE1
Tube: Tower Hill, London Bridge
Telephone: 020 7378 7031

Across the river from Dickens Inn is Terence Conran's oldest restaurant and it is fabulous: outstanding California–Italian food, slick service and incredible views from the terrace windows. It is expensive, though, and you must book in advance. Your reward is a meal to savour and long remember. **££££–£££££**

✕ Butler's Wharf Chop House

www.conran.com
The Butler's Wharf Building,
36e Shad Thames, SE1
Tube: Tower Hill
Telephone: 020 7403 3403

Terence Conran also owns this restaurant, and while you can't reserve a table on the terrace, do try for a window seat for those glorious Thames views. The menu features British food. While prices are high, you do have a choice between a simple dish at the bar, a reasonably priced set lunch or an extravagant dinner. **££–£££££**

✕ Chez Gérard

14 Trinity Square, EC3
Tube: Tower Hill
Telephone: 020 7480 5500

This chain of French restaurants, with charming Art Deco décor, remains popular for pleasant French food, especially the consistently good steak frites. **££–£££**

Dennis Severs House

www.dennissevershouse.co.uk
18 Folgate Street, Spitalfields, E1
Tube: Liverpool Street
Telephone: 020 7247 4013
Hours: Monday evenings (times vary); 2–5pm first and third Sunday of each month; 12 noon–2pm first and third Monday of each month,
Admission charge

This house is an 18th-century private townhouse turned museum. It is a time capsule. Exit onto Bishopsgate, walk left a few blocks to Folgate Street, then cross over for this unique and inspiring setting, a most intimate piece of theatre. Guests are escorted into candle-lit chambers from which, it would seem, their 18th- and 19th-century inhabitants have only just withdrawn. There might be clothes scattered about, a pair of glasses put down for a moment, a toy dropped on the carpet, a half-eaten pheasant tart sitting on the dining-room table, candles burning low… This is a unique opportunity to step back in time, connect your heart and mind with an earlier era and emerge knowing you have experienced something rare.

▪ SPITALFIELDS MARKET

Commercial Street, E1
Tube: Liverpool Street
Hours: 11am–3.30pm Monday–Friday; 10am–3pm Sunday
Free admission

In the late 17th century, French Huguenots fled persecution in their native country and settled in Spitalfields. Many were master weavers and dyers in the silk industry, and they helped the area to prosper. When the silk industry declined the area sunk into poverty.

In the 1880s, the area was infiltrated by thousands of Jewish immigrants fleeing the Russian pogroms, and at the end of the British Empire in the 20th century the cosmopolitan mix of the area was added to by an influx of Bengali immigrants.

Today, Spitalfields Market is a vibrant centre, and Sunday is the most popular market day.

From Dennis Severs House (see above) Spitalfields is just a short walk back towards Liverpool Street station on Bishopsgate. The graceful glass-covered market, its original frame built in 1893, is teeming with vendors, food stalls, music and people. It has been re-born to a New Age beat and its original flower-sellers and fruit-mongers are long gone.

Along with outrageous fashion design (both for sale and being worn) and all sorts of tarot readers, jewellery designers and stalls of the new and neon, you'll find a dizzying array of exciting food options: **stalls offer satay, sweet and savoury crêpes, falafel, tandoori and much more, which you buy and take to any vacant table**. This is a highly recommended, adventurous food stop. **£**

Hampton Court Palace

www.hrp.org.uk
East Molesey, Surrey, KT8
Train: Hampton Court (from London Waterloo, 30 minutes)
Telephone: 0870 752 7777
Hours: 30 March–26 October: 10.15am–6pm Monday, 9.30am–6pm Tuesday–Sunday; 27 October–29 March: 10.15am–4.30pm Monday, 9.30am–4.30pm Tuesday–Sunday; gardens open 7am–dusk all year round; closed 24–28 December
Admission charge

The 16th-century Hampton Court Palace is probably the most interesting royal residence of all. It was built by Cardinal Thomas Wolsey and expropriated by Henry VIII after the good cardinal's head was chopped off. This is a magnificent Tudor palace, set in extensive gardens and parkland on the banks of the Thames. It is wonderful to tour the Tudor kitchens, tennis courts, state apartments, king's apartments, Georgian apartments and to take your chances wandering the maze (children love this). The heyday of this palace was during Elizabethan times, but the present look is the work of Sir Christopher Wren (1632–1723). Some of the Tudor elements include the Anne Boleyn Gateway with its 16th-century clock, Clock Court and the Great Hall. What makes touring this palace exciting is that you have a sense of how royalty once lived within these walls – the kitchen alone is amazing, with its array of copper pots and pans, one for every possible purpose.

Hampton Court can also be reached by riverboat from Westminster, Richmond and Kingston piers (only in summer), but the journey is long. However, it is lovely to see the homes that line the river as you pass by, and snacks are available on board.

You can also take the bus from Victoria coach station. Look for bus numbers 111, 411, 216, 451 and 461. Hampton Court is 13 miles west of London, so you can do some sightseeing en route.

✂ EATING AT HAMPTON COURT PALACE

The **Tiltyard Gardens Café and Tearoom** is the best place to stop for lunch or tea right inside the palace grounds, and it is very pleasant. Expect to find soup and breads, hot dishes, sandwiches and fresh pastries. The food is fine and inexpensive. **£–££**

In the **Privy Kitchen Coffee Shop**, however, you can get coffee, tea, pastries and a light lunch, which might be all you need before returning to London. **£**

Two **ice-cream kiosks** can be found in the gardens during the summer months.

Windsor Castle

www.royal.gov.uk
Windsor, Surrey
Train: Windsor Royal (from London Paddington) or
Windsor Riverside (from London Waterloo)
Hours: 9.45am–4.15pm, November–February,
9.45am–5.15pm, March–October
Admission charge

Windsor Castle is the largest and oldest occupied castle in the world, and is home to Her Majesty Queen Elizabeth II. The castle's dramatic site encapsulates 900 years of history, and its magnificent state rooms and works of art reflect the tastes of successive kings and queens. In 1992, a devastating fire destroyed or damaged more than a hundred rooms. The highly acclaimed restoration work, completed in 1997, is a testament to the extraordinary skills of some of the finest craftsmen in Europe. You are sure to enjoy exploring the castle as well as meandering through the charming town of Royal Windsor.

The best way to travel to Windsor is by train from London Waterloo or London Paddington. For train times phone 08457 484950. Green Line coach services leave often from Victoria coach station in London, and several tour companies operate a daily service collecting from many London hotels.

If you are taking the train from Waterloo you will arrive at Riverside station. Keep the castle on your left as you walk up to the town centre (and castle entrance). If you are taking the train from Paddington and changing at Slough, you will arrive at Windsor Royal station. As you emerge the castle will be in front of you. Both trains take about the same amount of time.

You can combine a trip to Windsor in the morning with Hampton Court Palace (see page 41) in the afternoon as both are in the same locality. Also, Runnymede, where King John was forced to sign the Magna Carta in 1215, is near Windsor.

✕ EATING IN WINDSOR

There are no eating facilities in the castle, but in the town of Windsor you will find many restaurants, pubs and cafés. If you have arrived at Riverside station, your walk to the castle will take you past a number of these, but they are mostly chains.

If you have arrived at Windsor Royal station, you will alight into a delightful complex. Built by Great Western Railway in 1897 to commemorate Queen Victoria's Diamond Jubilee, it was completely refurbished in 1997 into an award-winning shopping destination. A soaring glass-covered roof shelters the shops and eateries beneath. You will find numerous places to have a meal, snack or cappuccino. **£–££**

Heading up the High Street and across the street onto Castle Hill you will pass a pub called the **Horse and Groom** at 4 Castle Hill (01753 830172). This is a personal favourite as the interior is so charmingly British (to an American like me!) and the pub food is good and reasonably priced. The menu is predictable and satisfying and includes soups, sandwiches, jacket potatoes and cream teas. **£–££**

MAJOR ATTRACTIONS

A banquet of extraordinary, interesting and beautiful marvels will keep you coming back for seconds... Soar above the city on the London Eye, attend a symphony at the Barbican Centre, stroll along untamed Hampstead Heath or get scared witless in the Chamber of Horrors at Madame Tussauds.

The London Eye is one of the capital's foremost attractions, thanks to the superlative views it provides over the heart of the city and beyond.

The Barbican is the London home of the London Symphony Orchestra. It is also a magnificent cultural showcase and offers a constant breathtaking flow of extraordinary film, theatre, dance, music, literature, art and design. Three theatres (Barbican Hall, Barbican Theatre and The Pit), plus galleries and outdoor areas, make this an exciting entertainment arena. The Barbican is built on levels, with an inner courtyard that is an oasis of peace where you can take afternoon tea or other meals, weather permitting.

Children aged 5–11 will enjoy the Barbican Cinema Club every Saturday in Cinema One. Call the Cinema hotline 020 7382 7000 for information and booking.

✂ EATING AT THE BARBICAN

Searcy's Restaurant and Lounge Bar on the Library Floor, Level 2, is open Monday to Friday 12 noon–3pm and 5–10.30pm, Saturday 5–10.30pm, Sunday 12 noon–3pm and 5pm until performance time. Wonderful, high-quality, well-presented meals are turned out here. Reservations can be made on 020 7588 3008. **£££–££££**.

The Lounge bar also serves excellent value 'Bowl Food', the Barbican's equivalent to bar food. **££**

At the **Balcony Bistro** on the Balcony Floor, Level 1, there is a relaxed atmosphere and friendly service, with a lovely view over the reflecting pool. Open Monday to Saturday 12 noon–10.30pm, Sundays 12 noon until performance time. Telephone 020 7628 3331. **££–£££**

There are **Coffee Points**

on Level 0 and Level -1, where sandwiches, cakes and good quality coffee are served pre-performance and at the intervals. **£**

The **Waterside Café** on the Ground Floor, Level 0, is open Monday to Saturday 9.30am–7.30pm and Sunday 10.30am–7.30pm. Early Bird dining specials (5–6pm) include a complimentary soft drink or coffee. Newly refurbished, the self-service café is sleek and stylish with plenty of options, from Thai beef to warm panini with mozzarella and basil. The dessert area almost always has awesome banoffee pie. The menu changes with the seasons. **£–££**

Finally, the **Concert Café** on the Balcony Floor, Level 1, serves light snacks and drinks, pre-performance and at intervals. It's a walk-up counter in the lobby area (with ample seating). **£**

Covent Garden

www.covent-garden.market.co.uk
Tube: Covent Garden
Hours: Shops are open 10am–6pm
Free admission

Although the era of Eliza Doolittle has long gone, Covent Garden remains a charming, hip, interesting and colourful marketplace. Of course it has changed from when Eliza sold violets to the swells entering the Opera House, but with the stunning renovation of the Royal Opera House; the daily markets offering food, crafts and funk; the Monday Jubilee antiques markets; and the Tuesday to Saturday crafts fair – and of course the non-stop street entertainment which can be very very good – you have an area of terrific entertainment. On a recent visit we were thrilled to hear a soaring contralto voice from the lower gallery and gladly tossed a few coins into the hat in admiration. We discovered later that the young woman was singing to pay for her voice lessons, and her mother was singing in the Royal Opera House next door.

Lovely boutiques and speciality shops offer decorative items for self and home. Surrounding the market are more shops and dance and art studios. Paul Smith has a nice branch here of his classic clothing line, and the popular Tin Tin Shop is on Floral Street.

Street performers entertain the crowds daily in Covent Garden

Within Covent Garden are several places for coffee, pastries and light meals. These are all fine and very convenient but not particularly special (unless you're freezing and holding a hot cup of coffee feels heavenly). Below are some decent places, worth the few paces they take to reach.

✗ Christopher's

www.christophersgrill.com
18 Wellington Street, WC2
Tube: Covent Garden, Charing Cross
Telephone: 020 7240 4222

You have three choices here depending upon your appetite and/or mood. The bar area is in the basement, the street level is where oysters, fresh salads and other dishes are served in a bistro-style setting, while serious diners ascend an elaborate, baroque, corkscrew-shaped stone staircase one floor to a pair of Italianate dining rooms.

The food served in the dining rooms is modern American, or very close to it. California wines are featured. On Saturday and Sunday brunch, very popular, is served 12 noon–4pm (**££**). A pre-theatre set two-course dinner is available (**££**).

Prices are lower in the street-level bar so you may wish to try that before the main dining room as the food all comes from the same kitchen. Booking is wise. **££–££££**

✕ Livebait

21 Wellington Street, WC2
Tube: Covent Garden, Charing Cross
Telephone: 020 7836 7161

If you love fresh fish then this is a place to try. The dining room is tiled in black and white and the staff is friendly. Known for the high quality of their fish and seafood and their superb cooking, they are almost always busy and cheerful. The prices are a bit steep, but they usually have a menu for children or a special offer. **£££**

✕ Diana's Diner

39 Endell St, WC2
Tube: Covent Garden
Telephone: 020 7240 0272

If you are looking for a casual meal and sometimes don't mind sharing a bench you can have very large portions of homemade pies, omelettes, grills and chips in this friendly little café. **£–££**

✕ Mode, WC2

57 Endell Street
Tube: Covent Garden
Telephone: 020 7240 8085

Nice Italian sandwiches and cheeses from nearby Neal's Yard make for a tasty lunch in a laid-back atmosphere. **£–££**

✕ Frank's

52 Neal Street, WC2
Tube: Covent Garden
Telephone: 020 7836 6345

Frank's serves all-day breakfasts, pasta and omelettes and other light dishes in this Italian café/sandwich bar. It can be hard to find a table in this busy café, so, if you can, come before or after the busy lunch hour. No credit cards or traveller's cheques. **£**

✕ Neal Street Restaurant

26 Neal Street, WC2
Tube: Covent Garden
Telephone: 020 7836 8368

This is the flagship restaurant of Antonio Carluccio, master of mushrooms (but talented in other areas as well). The dining room features work by artists such as David Hockney, Frank Stella and others. A small bar area downstairs is a pleasant place to have a pre-dinner drink. Everything on the menu is wonderful, and the choices can be as exotic or traditional as you wish. Booking advised. **££££**

Adjacent to the restaurant is **Carluccio's take-away deli and grocery**. Their small jars of truffle oil make wonderful gifts. If dining in the restaurant would blow your budget, try any Carluccio's Caffé, which are flourishing under his management and dedication to quality food at friendly prices.

✕ Food For Thought

31 Neal Street, WC2
Tube: Covent Garden
Telephone: 020 7836 0239

The menu is completely vegetarian at this busy café, which always has good food and daily changing specials. They also offer vegan and wheat-free options. As it is usually so busy, this is not the place for a leisurely lunch (unless you wish to arrive well before or after the lunch crowd). The take-away counter is great if you want to keep moving on to the next destination. I am not a vegetarian but find the food here absolutely wonderful. **£**

✕ Neal's Yard Bakery & Tearoom

6 Neal's Yard, WC2
Tube: Covent Garden
Telephone: 020 7836 5199

Order your pleasure from the superb organic co-op bakery on the ground floor then take it upstairs to enjoy in the (sort of) ramshackle dining area. No credit cards. **£**

✕ Mon Plaisir

www.monplaisir.co.uk
21 Monmouth Street, WC2
Tube: Covent Garden, Leicester Square
Telephone: 020 7836 7243

This restaurant has been here a very long time, and its imitation of a Paris bistro is accurate enough to keep satisfied customers coming back. It can be expensive when you order à la carte, but the set lunch is excellent value and the regional French cooking is truly good. It is also a wonderful and exceptionally good value choice for a pre-theatre supper; you need to vacate your table by 7.30pm. This place is popular and booking is strongly recommended. **££–£££**

✕ Monmouth Coffee Company

27 Monmouth St, WC2
Tube: Covent Garden,
Leicester Square
Telephone: 020 7379 3516

This branch of the coffee company is rather better than others if you enjoy the atmosphere of an 18th-century coffee house with cramped wooden booths; daily newspapers are offered to read while you sip. You can get a good breakfast here as well as other light meals. **£–££**

✕ Maggiore's

33 King Street, WC2
Tube: Covent Garden, Charing Cross
Telephone: 020 7379 9696

Not far from the centre of the action at Covent Garden, Maggiore's restaurant is a charming choice for either lunch or dinner. Especially nice is the central conservatory area with a glass roof – beautiful in the summertime. During winter, a blazing fire in a handsome brick fireplace makes the room cosy. The staff is most welcoming, and the service attentive and pleasant. It has a loyal clientèle so booking is advised. **££–£££**

✕ All Bar One

19 Bedford Street,
Tube: Covent Garden, Charing Cross
Telephone: 020 7557 7941

This is one of many All Bar One restaurants, all very popular with a young crowd. Wines and champagnes are prominently described on the menu and the food offerings vary from sandwiches to main courses to platters to share. They also serve good breakfasts that include components such as sweetcorn fritters, smoked salmon and fried eggs on toasted ciabatta bread. **££**

✕ Paul French Bakery

29 Bedford Street, WC2
Tube: Covent Garden, Charing Cross
Telephone: 020 7836 3304

After you have admired the woven baskets heaped with freshly made breads, cakes, croissants and other delicious French bakery treats, you'll probably have an appetite. So pick up something to take with you, or, better still, go through the interior glass doors and treat yourself to a breakfast pastry, a sumptuous lunch or a light dinner in the small café. Wonderful coffees and teas plus wine are available, and please don't skip dessert. **££**

✕ Porters English Restaurant

www.porters.uk.com
17 Henrietta Street, WC2
Tube: Covent Garden, Charing Cross
Telephone: 020 7836 6466

This is a wonderful choice for English food at affordable prices. The two-course lunch, served 12 noon–4.30pm, is good value. They serve grills, onion and ale soup, 'olde English fish pie', bangers and mash and roast beef with Yorkshire pudding. There are also steamed puddings for afters, and a traditional tea is served 2.30–5.30pm. The restaurant was opened in 1979 by the 7th Earl of Bradford, and the banana and ginger pudding recipe is from Lady Bradford. Booking is essential. **££**

Greenwich

www.greenwichguide.co.uk
Tube: Greenwich North
Train: Overland service to Greenwich
Hours: All day, everyday
Free admission

A 15-minute train ride from Charing Cross is the easiest and quickest way to travel to Greenwich. Other options include cruises on the Thames from Westminster Pier (Tube: Westminster), Charing Cross Pier (Tube: Embankment) and Tower Pier (Tube: Tower Hill), which take from an hour or more each way. The Docklands Light Railway (which is a tourist attraction in itself) will take you to Greenwich from Tower Gateway (Tube: Tower Hill) or Bank. The blue and white carriages pass above the Isle of Dogs and other sights before arriving at Greenwich and the *Cutty Sark*.

As you enter the old village from the train station you will come to a **weekend antique market**. It's anyone's guess what will be on offer at any given time, but it's always worth a browse to find out. Continuing to the intersection you will see ahead of you another large market with mostly outdoor stalls. The building holds shops of New Age trinkets on the ground floor and older vintage items upstairs, but the outdoor, partially covered market is lively, noisy and a lot more fun. Furniture, clothing, Victoriana, secondhand books, stamps, bottles and medals – a real jumble is to be found here, among which it is almost always possible to find something for very little money. On the first Sunday of each month (weather permitting in winter) there is a farmers' market set up. You will find fresh, unusual breads, olives, mustards, oils, vinegars and spices, cheeses and meats, jams, chutneys and yogurt drinks, coffees and teas, wines, quiches and pot pies, tiny pizzas and enormous sausages – and much more. You can easily put together a portable meal here. Some of the vendors come over from France and Belgium to sell their wares. There is also a lovely flower stand here on the weekends.

Continuing towards the main section of town, and the landmarks described below, you will find a **covered market-place** selling crafts, prints and books, jewellery, clothing and the wooden clocks that make perfect souvenirs. The reasonably priced clocks come in classic shapes and many sizes. Ringing the market are small indoor shops with crafts and clothing.

As you approach the river you will see the *Cutty Sark*, which you can board and tour (admission charged). Built in 1869, this is the last of the tea-clippers who plied the trade until the 1920s. The exhibits below decks show the history of sail and the Pacific trade routes. In addition, Sir Francis Chichester's *Gipsy Moth* is on display to your left, and if you bear right at the River Thames, you can walk to the museums, park and observatory.

Since Greenwich was the centre of seafaring when Britain ruled the seas, it is the home of the **Royal Naval College**, the **National Maritime Museum** and the **Old Royal Observatory**. GMT – Greenwich Mean Time – is the basis of standard timekeeping throughout the world. Since 1884, Greenwich has been the location for the zero point used in reckoning terrestrial longitudes. So, this is the place to set your watch to the right time.

Greenwich also has an extremely rich royal history, with Greenwich Palace being the birthplace of many Tudor kings and queen's, including Mary Queen of Scots and her arch-rival Queen Elizabeth I.

■ NATIONAL MARITIME MUSEUM

www.nmm.ac.uk
Romney Road, SE10
Train: Greenwich
Telephone: 020 8858 4422
Hours: 10am–5pm (till 6pm in the summer months); closed 24–26 December
Free admission

Here you can view the history of Britain's sea power from the earliest days until the 20th century. The stories of thousands of battles, countless victories and innumerable casualties are told in displays of cannons, ship models, paintings and oddities. Nelson's Trafalgar coat is on exhibit, clearly showing the fatal bullet hole in the left shoulder.

The **Regatta Café** is bright and cheerful with wood floors, modern chandeliers, floor-to-ceiling windows and nautical touches. This is a Milburn-catered establishment so expect the same good food as in the Victoria & Albert Museum (see page 93), among others. It is open every day during museum hours and is accessible also from Greenwich Park. Morning and afternoons offer cakes, biscuits, scones and sandwiches and 12 noon–2.30pm they add hot dishes, salads and desserts. **£–££**

On the airy and open mezzanine floor, among some exhibits, is a place to sit down, have a hot or cold drink and a snack: the **Upper Deck**. They feature a child-friendly box (also offered in the Regatta) of sandwich, biscuit, fruit and toy. **£**

■ ROYAL OBSERVATORY

www.rog.nmm.ac.uk
Greenwich Park, SE10
Train: Greenwich
Telephone: 020 8858 4422
Hours: 10am–5pm (till 6pm in the summer months); closed 24–26 December
Free admission

The original home of Greenwich Mean Time has the largest refracting telescope in the UK and a wonderful collection of astronomical instruments and historic timekeepers. It is the home of all five of Harrison's clocks and a must-see for anyone interested in (early) navigation. Sir Christopher Wren's genius can be found in the Octagon Room he designed. You can stand astride the meridian and set your watch precisely by the falling time ball.

■ QUEEN'S HOUSE

www.nmm.ac.uk
Romney Road, SE10
Train: Greenwich
Telephone: 020 8858 4422
Hours: 10am–5pm (till 6pm in
the summer months); closed
24–26 December
Free admission

Built by Inigo Jones in 1616, Queen's House is a stunning example of this architect's style. The first cantilevered staircase was built here, and a wonderful collection of royal and marine paintings and objets d'art make this a wonderful place to visit.

■ ROYAL NAVAL COLLEGE

www.greenwichfoundation.org.uk
Greenwich Park, SE10
Train: Greenwich
Telephone: 020 8269 4747
Hours: Grounds: 8am–6pm;
College 10am–5pm; closed
24–26 December
Free admission

The Greenwich Palace stood on this site from 1422 until 1640. In 1696, Sir Christopher Wren designed the enormous four-block Royal Naval College, with blocks named after King Charles, Queen Anne, King William and Queen Mary. This is where Lord Nelson lay in state in 1805. Also here is the Georgian chapel of St Peter and St Paul.

✕ EATING IN GREENWICH

You will not go hungry in Greenwich. Besides the weekend food stalls and market food, there are many varied established places that feed the locals.

✕ The Coach and Horses

13 Greenwich Market, SE10
Train: Greenwich, Maze Hill
Telephone: 020 8293 0880

This pub sits on one corner of the bustling market. Besides tables and chairs for dining, there is a cosy fireplace with comfy sofas and armchairs. A menu of hot dishes, sandwiches and snacks is available. Children are welcome. **£–££**

✕ Greenwich Market Food Court

www.greenwichmarket.net
Greenwich Market, SE10
Train: Greenwich, Maze Hill
Telephone: 020 8293 3110

Although there is nowhere to sit down and eat, the fresh food sold here is irresistible.

You could pick something up to munch on as you browse, such as a hot beef sandwich, or buy something delicious to enjoy later – cheese, bread, cold meats, patés, and much, much more. Various prices.

✕ Greenwich Park Café

Nelson Road, SE10
Train: Greenwich, Maze Hill, Blackheath

This self-service restaurant is in an elegant Edwardian building that dates back to 1905. Delicious hot and cold food is on offer. **£**

✕ La Cucina

1 Nelson Road, SE10
Train: Greenwich, Maze Hill
Telephone: 020 8858 8424

Bright and modern, a range of pizza, fish and pasta is served here. **££–£££**

✕ The Mitre

291 Greenwich High Road, Greenwich, SE10
Train: Greenwich
Telephone: 020 8293 0037

The food in this pleasant pub is good and the attached atrium dining room is lovely on a sunny day. You can have a hearty hot lunch here or a simple sandwich. **£–££**

✕ Noodle Time

10–11 Nelson Road, SE10
Train: Greenwich
Telephone: 020 8293 5263

The format here is simple. You are shown to your table (bench seating) and the menu is under glass. Your waiter will give you an order pad and a pencil and you circle the numbers of the items you want to order, including drinks. Within minutes you will be served. All the dishes are extraordinarily generous, authentic and delicious, and very, very cheap. Also good are the fresh juices. Bar service and children's menu are also available. No credit cards. **£**

✕ Pistachios

15 Nelson Road, SE10
Train: Greenwich
Telephone: 020 8853 0602

A wide variety of luncheon choices as well as an all-day breakfast are available in this little café. There is a bright atrium dining area in the rear. Children are welcome. There is also bar service. **££**

✕ Thai Chung

8 Nelson Road, SE10
Train: Greenwich
Telephone: 020 8858 8588

Inexpensive prices will buy a meal of almost any Thai dish you can think of in a pleasant atmosphere. They offer all kinds of noodles, Pad Thai and so on. **£**

✕ The Trafalgar Tavern

www.trafalgartavern.co.uk
6 Park Row, SE10
Train: Greenwich
Telephone: 020 8858 2507

Famous for its whitebait, which has been served since Victorian times, standard pub food is on offer here at reasonable prices. **££**

Hampstead Heath
Tube: Hampstead (Edgware branch of Northern Line)
Hours: All day, every day
Free admission

Hampstead Heath is an 800-acre expanse of parkland, woodland, heath, meadowland and ponds. Although it is four miles north of central London it is only 20 minutes by tube from Piccadilly Circus. Until 1907, when the tube came to the village of Hampstead, it was very popular with musicians, scientists, artists and writers, who thrived in the leafy, country atmosphere.

The village retains much of its original charm to this day, with a mixture of Regency and Georgian houses, historic pubs, chic boutiques (along Flask Walk), outdoor cafés, and, of course, Hampstead Heath, a large park offering panoramic views of the city. It is delightful to sit on one of the park benches and view the entire city from this high vantage point. The original village on the side of a hill still has the old alleys, steps, courts and groves that are lovely for strolling.

Londoners today enjoy the area for craft and antique fairs, sunbathing, kite flying, pond fishing, swimming, picnicking and jogging. Near Kenwood Lake (in the northern section of the park), symphony performances are held on summer evenings, and in Waterlow Park (northeast corner) you can attend ballets, operas and comedies at the Grass Theatre during June and July. You can lose the 21st century totally when you find yourself wandering through Church Row, Admiral's Walk and Flask Walk. Places to visit in the area follow.

KEATS HOUSE

www.keatshouse.org.uk
Keats Grove, Hampstead, NW3
Tube: Belsize Park, Hampstead
Telephone: 020 7435 2062
Hours: 12 noon–4pm
Tuesday–Sunday
Admission charge

This Regency House is where poet John Keats (1795–1821) wrote 'Ode to a Nightingale' (under a plum tree in the garden) and 'Ode on a Grecian Urn'. Some of his manuscripts and letters are on display as well as a collection of his personal possessions.

FREUD MUSEUM

www.freud.org.uk
20 Maresfield Gardens, NW3
Tube: Finchley Road
Telephone: 020 7435 2002
Hours: 12 noon–5pm
Wednesday–Sunday
Admission charge

You can see Sigmund Freud's (1856–1939) famous psychoanalytic couch as well as furniture, letters, photographs, paintings and personal effects (including those of his daughter, Anna). The founder of psychoanalysis, Freud lived, worked and died here after escaping from Nazi-occupied Vienna.

FENTON HOUSE

www.nationaltrust.org/places/fentonhouse
3 Hampstead Grove, NW3
Tube: Hampstead
Telephone: 020 7435 3471
Hours: 2–5pm Wednesday–Friday; 11am–5pm weekends and bank holidays
Admission charge

This National Trust property is located on the west side of Hampstead Grove, just north of Hampstead Village, and was built in 1693. On view are early keyboard musical instruments, 18th-century English, German and French porcelain and a collection of paintings and furniture.

BURGH HOUSE

New End Square, NW3
Tube: Hampstead
Telephone: 020 7431 0144
Hours: 12 noon–5pm Wednesday–Sunday; 2–5pm bank holidays
Free admission

This Queen Anne home, dating from 1703, is located in the centre of the village and was once the residence of the daughter and son-in-law of the novelist Rudyard Kipling (1865–1936). Today it is home to local art exhibits, recitals, concerts, lectures and various public meetings, and is also the location for local societies, such as the Hampstead Music Club and the Hampstead Scientific Society.

The Hampstead Museum in Burgh House depicts local history and has a room of reproductions of paintings by John Constable (1776–1837), who lived nearby and who is buried in the local parish church.

⚔ EATING AT BURGH HOUSE

In the basement Monica's Specialist Caterers run the **Burgh House Buttery** (020 7431 2516). Morning coffee, lunch, afternoon tea and snacks are available, and in fine weather customers can eat on the terrace overlooking the Heath. **£–££**

⚔ Cucina
45A South End Road, NW3
Tube: Hampstead, Belsize Park
Telephone: 020 7435 7814

A modest frontage leads to a much larger place inside. Cucina is cheerful and delightful, with a champagne bar. The chefs prepare outstanding adventurous

dishes and the prices are reasonable and the service above average. **£££**

⚔ The House on Rosslyn Hill
34 Rosslyn Hill, NW3
Tube: Hampstead
Telephone: 020 7435 8037

This is a bistro-style place that serves simple and good food such as pastas, salads and sausage and mash with terrific onion gravy. **££–£££**

⚔ Byrons
3A Downshire Hill, NW3
Tube: Hampstead, Belsize Park
Telephone: 020 7435 3544

The wonderful menu at Byrons features delicious and inventive seasonal combinations. The pretty dining room adds to the pleasure. **£££**

⚔ Zen W3
83 Hampstead High Street, NW3
Tube: Hampstead
Telephone: 020 7794 7863

The packed dining room is testimony to the excellence of the Chinese food at Zen. Everything is fresh, flavourful, complex and delicious. A special treat are the toffee apples and toffee bananas, hard to find outside Hong Kong. There are several other branches in London (and in Hong Kong, too). **££–£££**

✗ Louis Patisserie

32 Heath Street, NW3
Tube: Hampstead

A tempting window display of Middle European bakery specialities will lure you into this café. It's just a few steps away from the tube station. You can also take away the breads and pastries sold here. No credit cards. **£**

✗ Maison Blanc

www.maisonblanc.co.uk
62 Hampstead High Street, NW3
Tube: Hampstead
Telephone: 020 7431 8338

Here you can indulge in anything from handmade quiche to tarte au citron. **£**

London Aquarium

www.londonaquarium.co.uk
County Hall, Westminster Bridge Road, SE1
Tube: Waterloo, Westminster, Embankment,
Charing Cross
Telephone: 020 7967 8000
Hours: 10am–6pm (till 7pm during school holidays)
Admission charge

The aquarium is on three levels complete with appropriate lighting and sounds. The Atlantic, for example, features a huge three-storey tank filled with sharks, stingrays and other awesome creatures, and the Discovery Zone is a hands-on experience where you can touch starfish, crabs and more.

✗ EATING AT LONDON AQUARIUM

The on-site café is adjacent to the aquarium. The offerings are mediocre and overpriced, but will do in a pinch. I suggest taking your snack outside so you can enjoy the view. **££**

✗ For dining options beyond the London Aquarium, please see the
Royal Festival Hall on pages 66-67.

London Eye

www.londoneye.com
Jubilee Gardens, SE1
Tube: Waterloo, Westminster, Embankment,
Charing Cross
Telephone: 0870 5000 600 (advance bookings)
Hours: 9.30am–10pm (summer); 9.30am–8pm (winter)
Admission charge

At Jubilee Gardens, South Bank, a 135-metre-high Ferris wheel
– the London Eye – has been built on the River Thames by
British Airways, and is the highest observation wheel in the
world. Exit Waterloo station, bear right and the Eye will be before
you. Or alight at Embankment north of the river and walk across

*The London Eye
provides the best
views of London,
both through the
day and at night*

the Thames by way of one of the new Hungerford Millennium footbridges (on either side of Charing Cross railway bridge).

A complete rotation of the London Eye takes about 30 minutes in glass-walled cabins that can accommodate up to 25 people each. The wheel moves so slowly that it does not need to stop to allow passengers to get on and off. You fly over the heart of London and on a lovely day you can see forever.

 EATING AT LONDON EYE

Just before the entrance to the Eye and the Aquarium you can enjoy coffee, snacks and sandwiches at **Costa** Coffee. (All the Costa Coffees are good.) Sit at one of the tables sheltered beneath a marquee, and get a great view of Big Ben for free. **£**

 For dining options beyond the London Eye, please see the Royal Festival Hall on pages 66–67.

London Zoo

www.londonzoo.co.uk
Outer Circle, Regent's Park, NW1
Tube: Camden Town
Telephone: 020 7722 3333
Hours: 10am–5.30pm (summer); 10am–4pm (winter)
Admission charge

Home to over 8,000 animals, this is one of the world's largest zoos, and is certainly the oldest (founded in 1826). Special features include Moonlight World, a children's zoo, Bear Mountain, Web of Life and a Lifewatch Conservation Centre. Children will enjoy feeding the pigs, watching the penguins at feeding time, and trying to choose where to start as there are so many wonderful activities waiting to be explored.

EATING AT LONDON ZOO

Four restaurants and cafés are located throughout the zoo and vary from casual, sit-down waiter service to cafeteria-style to food carts. The food is simple, child-

friendly and really quite good. £

✕ As London Zoo is within Regent's Park, please see pages 104–105 for further dining options.

London Planetarium

www.london-planetarium.com
Marylebone Road, NW1
Tube: Baker St
Telephone: 0870 400 3000 (advance bookings)
Hours: 12.30–5.30pm Monday–Friday; 10.30am–5.30pm
weekends and school holidays
Admission charge, combined tickets with Madame
Tussauds available

The star shows last 30 minutes and take place every 30 minutes Monday to Friday from 12.30pm to 5pm (last show). Earlier times, from 10.30am, are in effect on Saturdays, Sundays and school holidays. Visitors can experience a virtual reality trip through the solar system, galaxies and beyond, and wander through the interactive space zones. You could combine this very educational, but extremely fun, visit with one to Madame Tussaud's; see below.

✕ As London Planetarium is on the edge of Regent's Park, please see pages 104–105 for further dining options.

Madame Tussauds

www.madame-tussauds.com
Marylebone Road, NW1
Tube: Baker St
Telephone: 0870 400 3000 (advance bookings)
Hours: 12.30–5.30pm Monday–Friday; 10.30am–5.30pm
weekends and school holidays
Admission charge, combined tickets with London
Planetarium available

Madame Tussaud was a Frenchwoman who attended the court of Versailles and learned her craft in France. In 1802 she moved her original museum of wax figures from Paris to England, and it has been on its present site since 1884. Although her exhibitions have been copied and imitated around the world, none compare to the realism and imagination you see here.

Madame herself moulded the features of Benjamin Franklin; all the rest have been painstakingly created by others with breathtaking reality in the results. You will see almost every famous person you have ever heard of in this museum, as well as experience the chilling Chamber of Horrors with its instruments of death and figures of the unfortunate victims.

Features include 'time-taxis' which allow you to see and *hear* 'Shakespeare', be received by Queen Elizabeth I, feel and smell the Great Fire of 1666 that destroyed London, and enjoy a musical ride 'The Spirit of London' with special effects.

✖ EATING AT MADAME TUSSAUDS

In the Grand Hall you will find a **café** tucked between the political figures and the Chamber of Horrors. Tables are set up for you to enjoy your snack from the cafeteria-style display. **£**

✖ As Madame Tussauds is on the edge of Regent's Park, please see pages 104–105 for further dining options.

✖ Villandry Food Hall and Restaurant

www.villandry.com
170 Great Portland Street, W1
Tube: Great Portland Street
Telephone: 020 7631 3131

I call this establishment a mini-Harrods Food Hall. It is a feast for the senses on a small scale, and a jewel of a find in this neighbourhood.

It's an easy walk from Madame Tussaud's and the Planetarium. The food hall contains chocolates, fresh produce, an amazing variety of French and English cheeses, fresh fish and meats, flowers, small gifts and a take-away counter of delicious hot and cold small meals or snacks.

For full meals, eat in the

Villandry restaurant. Restaurant hours are 12 noon–3pm and 6–10.30pm Monday to Saturday and 11.30am–4pm Sunday. For lighter fare and breakfast, try the bar, whose hours are 8am–11.30pm Monday to Friday, 9am–11.30pm on Saturday and 4–9.30pm on Sunday. Take-away prices in the food hall are budget to inexpensive (**£–££**) while meals in the restaurant cost a little more (**££–£££**).

✖ Patisserie Valerie at Maison Sagne

www.patisserie-valerie.co.uk
105 Marylebone High Street, W1
Tube: Baker Street, Bond Street
Telephone: 020 7935 6240

I love this place. Established in 1926, the pastries are the stuff of dreams if you are fond of chocolate and whipped cream. The lunches are very good, and the cakes and confections are amazing. Often there are wedding and other special occasion cakes on display and these are works of art.

It is a popular and stylish oasis for weary shoppers, and they can often be seen enjoying their pastry with a flute of champagne (£4.50 per glass).

This, or one of the other branches of Patisserie Valerie, should be experienced at least once. The original branch is on Old Compton Street in Soho (0202 7437 3466). The Knightsbridge branch (020 7823 9971) near Harrods, at 215 Brompton Road, gets a special buzz on Sundays when an international crowd surges in after services in the Brompton Oratory across the road. There are also branches in Kensington, Covent Garden and Belgravia. **£–££**

✖ Giraffe

6–8 Blandford Street, W1
Tube: Baker Street, Bond Street
Telephone: 020 7935 2333

In funky surroundings you can enjoy international food that is well prepared, unusual and often cooked with organic ingredients. Children enjoy the hamburgers and fries, and everyone else can go for one of the salads, stir-fries, pastas or filling sandwiches and wraps. The menu is large and eclectic and the prices reasonable. It is also convenient for The Wallace Collection (see page 20). **£–££**

Royal Albert Hall

www.royalalberthall.com
Kensington Gore, SW7
Tube: South Kensington, Gloucester Road
Telephone: 020 7589 8212
Hours: Box office open 9am–9pm
Admission: All events are individually priced

A 'great centrall hall' for public performances was the brainchild of Queen Victoria's husband Prince Albert. Albert, sadly, died 10 years before it opened, but it took his name in his honour. So many wonderful events take place in the Royal Albert Hall, and the location is so beautiful, that you may wish to access the website above to get a listing of what is happening. Since the hall's opening concert in 1871, over 150,000 performances have taken place there. The wildly popular Proms (the musical programmes that take place during late summer) can be difficult to book, but there are many other offerings, from popular vocalists to championship ballroom dancing competitions. (Mastercard and Visa are accepted for bookings.) Be sure to enjoy the ornate, over-the-top memorial to Prince Albert, which his grieving widow, Queen Victoria, had built in his honour (opposite the main entrance, in Kensington Gardens).

The Royal Albert Hall hosts the ever-popular Proms

✕ EATING IN THE ROYAL ALBERT HALL

The restaurants within the Royal Albert Hall open two hours before performances.

For the **Elgar Room Restaurant** (no smoking), enter via Door 8. Book by calling 020 7589 8212. This is fine dining in an elegant, sumptuous setting on the Circle level. **££–£££**

For the brasserie, the **Victoria Room** (no smoking), enter via Door 2. This is a stylish self-service restaurant on the Circle level, and in addition to the reasonably priced pasta dishes, salads and sandwiches you also get, for free, views over Kensington Gardens and the Albert Memorial. An affordable, delicious pre-performance stop. **£–££**

The **Champagne Bar** on the Grand Tier (via Door 2) serves champagnes, wines, spirits, beers and light snacks, and the remaining bars on the other levels open 45 minutes before each performance and during the intervals.

Alcoholic and non-alcoholic beverages, snacks and sandwiches are available in the **North Circle Bar**, **Lanson Arena Bar**, **West Arena Foyer** (no smoking), **Porch Bars** at Doors 4 and 9, **Ground Floor Bars** at Doors 6 and 7, **Victoria Bar** and **Second Tier Bar**. **£**

Royal Festival Hall
www.rfh.org.uk
South Bank, SE1
Tube: Embankment, Waterloo
Telephone: 020 7960 4242
Hours: 10am–10.30pm
Admission free, but most concerts are charged

This is one of London's most important concert halls, offering spacious foyers with bars, cafeterias, a restaurant, a bookshop and an on-going programme of live music and art exhibitions. What better place to be on a rainy Sunday? If you happen to be there on a sunny day, also take in the nearby London Eye (see page 60). If you opt to travel by tube via Embankment you can walk across the Thames via one of the new Hungerford Millennium footbridges and enjoy the view, and possibly a stiff breeze!

The Royal Festival Hall is one of a cluster of prominent cultural venues. Next to it are the Purcell Room, Hayward Gallery and Queen Elizabeth Hall, then the National Theatre and National Film Theatre (near Waterloo Bridge). The Embankment and Waterloo tubes serve these places as well. On summer weekends, outdoor events take place on the riverside terraces.

✕ EATING AT THE ROYAL FESTIVAL HALL

All the restaurants listed below are also convenient to the London Eye and the London Aquarium.

The People's Palace (020 7928 9999; www.capital-london.net/peoples-palace) on Level 3 is the perfect splurge. Wonderful modern British food (with influences of Modern European and North African), plus the lovely views, make this a treat. Lunchtime is 12 noon–3pm; dinner is 5.30–11pm (closed for dinner on bank holidays). **£££–££££**

On level 1, opposite the box office, is **51 Café** (020 7921 0948) serving snacks and coffee 9am–9pm, seven days a week. For lunch and dinner, separate food stations offer Indian, Italian and traditional English food, as well as salads, sandwiches and desserts. **£–££**

In the Main Foyer, Level 2, is **EAT** (020 7921 0804), open 10am–10.15pm, a self-service café with soups, sandwiches, snacks, salads and very good coffee. Wine is also available. **£**

The **Foyer Café** (020 7921 0948) in the Main Foyer, Level 2, is open daily 12 noon–2.30pm and, on evenings when there is a performance, 5–7.30pm for dinner. No smoking. **££**

✕ Oxo Tower Restaurant

www.oxotower.co.uk
Oxo Tower Wharf, Barge House Street, SE1
Tube: Blackfriars
Telephone: 020 7803 3888

The Oxo Tower Restaurant is a great place for summer dining, as the terrace provides spectacular views over the city, but the night-time view is just as good. The restaurant, whose design reflects a 1930s ocean-liner, has a reputation that goes before it and a wine list to match. **££££**

This historical theatre was built in 1856–8 by E. M. Barry and has recently had a major refurbishment. It is now more beautiful than ever. It is the London home of international opera and ballet, and it is thrilling to attend a performance here.

✗ EATING AT THE ROYAL OPERA HOUSE

To accompany a fine balletic or operatic performance there are several options within the Royal Opera House. However, all food must be pre-ordered; telephone 020 7212 9254.

The **Amphitheatre Restaurant**, situated on the top floor of the House, offers an excellent pre-theatre dinner in tranquil surroundings. **£££**. The **Vilar Floral Hall Balconies Restaurant** serves a similar menu but in more formal surroundings. **£££–££££**.

Those with a smaller appetite should head for the **Crush Room** where cold food is available or order snacks from the **Amphitheatre and Floral Hall Bars**. **££**

✗ As the Royal Opera House is in Covent Garden, please see pages 46–51 for further dining options.

On Sunday mornings at Speaker's Corner a 19th-century tradition carries on. Speakers have the chance to expound on any subject they wish and the fun is to catch the reactions of the crowd and the heckling that always accompanies a performance. You can hear anything from ridicule of royalty to sexual rhetoric and everything in between. Anyone can get up and speak. The ground rules do hold, however, that you can't blaspheme, be obscene or start a riot. This tradition began in 1855 (before the legal right to assembly was guaranteed in 1872) when a mob of 150,000 gathered to attack a proposed Sunday Trading Bill. Orators from all over the UK have been taking up their causes here ever since.

✕ Caffé Uno

11 Edgware Road, W2
Telephone: 020 7723 4898
Tube: Marble Arch

With a children's menu, and a Monday to Friday express lunch 12 noon–5pm at a budget price, plus opening hours from breakfast onwards, this is fine for a family dining choice. **£–££**

✕ SALT

13 Edgware Road, W2
Telephone: 020 7402 8012
Tube: Marble Arch

Open from 8am until late in the evening, this new bar and restaurant serves inexpensive pub food and sandwiches in the downstairs Whiskey Bar, while an à la carte menu is available upstairs. Trendy atmosphere. **££–£££**

Speaker's Corner often draws the crowds on a Sunday morning

MARKETS AND ANTIQUES

Everything from soup to silver can be found somewhere in one of London's myriad markets. Whether browsing colourful stalls, prowling the speciality shops or bravely heading for pre-dawn foraging at Bermondsey, you will find relics and rejects, treasures and kitsch, and be greatly in need of sustenance along the way.

Portobello Road in Notting Hill is perfect for browsing, and you never know what you might find among the stalls of antiques and bric à brac.

Alfies Antique Market

www.ealfies.com
13–25 Church Street, NW8
Tube: Edgware Road, Baker Street
Telephone: 020 7723 6066
Hours: 9am–6pm Tuesday–Saturday
Free admission

Exit the tube and walk to Edgware Road. Turn right and after about three blocks you come to Church Street. Turn right and you will be entering the street markets selling fruit and vegetables, meat and fish, and an assortment of cheap goods from toys to suitcases to zips to ladies' coats. Continue walking past some interesting antiques shops and you will come to Alfies, on the right-hand side of the street. Alfies is a warren of shops and stalls that meander over several floors via rickety staircases. There is a particularly nice secondhand bookshop on the second floor, and although many stalls specialize, some offer the whole range and you have to do some serious searching.

✗ EATING AT ALFIES

There is a **snack bar** on the upper level with budget prices for coffee and tea and a selection of hot food that is a delicious surprise as well as huge all-day breakfasts, pastries and sandwiches. There are tables on the roof for sunny-day dining. **£**

If you head south down Edgware Road you will come across plenty of Middle Eastern cafés selling falafel, kebabs and baklava. **£–££**

Bermondsey

www.bermondsey-square.com
Bermondsey Market , SE1
Tube: London Bridge, Tower Hill
Hours: 4am–12 noon Fridays
Free admission

The closest tube is London Bridge, but I always use Tower Hill. It is a longer route, but walking across Tower Bridge is worth it.

The views, the closeness to the Tower of London, the Thames … it's wonderful to see it all. Just keep walking another few blocks after crossing the bridge and you will see the market on your right. It's a brisk 20-minute walk from the tube stop. The market is in four areas: three of them are uncovered, separated only by narrow traffic lanes, and the fourth one is under cover across the street. The antique traders here are very professional and for the most part have a terrific stock; serious buyers arrive at 4am and do their searching with a torch, so the rest of us lazybones who get here about 7am will never see the 'best of the lot'. However, there is still much to look at and buy. Just try to come as early as you can. Haggling is the norm, but the traders here are, by and large, well established, honest and know the value of their wares. Particularly good buys are found in the silver stalls where most of the merchandize is piled up in an untidy heap and you have to rummage. This is where it pays to know what you are looking for. Most stallholders have silver hallmark books at hand and can look up a piece for you if you are uncertain of the maker or period.

✕ EATING AT BERMONDSEY

Several **trailers** are set up in the area to provide sustenance. Coffee, tea, hot chocolate and sweet buns (not very good) and a couple of sandwich offerings can be purchased and carried with you as you maintain the rhythm of your hunting instincts. I speak from experience, as on one early morning visit I had to feed my friend who absolutely would not leave the trading area for breakfast. She was happy with the hot bacon sandwich I carried to her and didn't miss a beat. **£**

✕ Rose's Dining Room
210 Bermondsey Street, SE1
Tube: London Bridge

Adjacent to the covered Bermondsey market is this hugely popular café that caters normally to local workmen but, on Fridays, to the antiques crowd. Since this is the only place in the area, it is noisy, crowded and fun. You will probably share a table but this adds to the spirit of the occasion. Most order the full English breakfast or the bacon sandwiches. This is a greasy spoon but the food tastes good. **£**

Camden Passage

www.islington.gov.uk/whatson
Camden Passage, N1
Tube: Angel
*Hours: 9am–3pm Wednesdays (General antiques
market); 9am–3pm Fridays (Booksellers' market);
9am–3pm Saturdays (General antiques & military market)*
Free admission

Exit the Angel tube station and go right. The market begins at the corner. Stalls veer off a little but you're never far from the main path. There are many treasures to be found here, but there is also a great deal of junk, so it's best to know what you are looking for. The popular vintage clothing store 'Annie's' is here. Most stalls are inside the various buildings, but a few are outside and they usually have some interesting things. It's also fun to chat with the stallholders. If you have time, wander around Upper Street and the interesting streets that lurk behind.

 Giraffe
29-31 Essex Road, N1
Tube: Angel
Telephone: 020 7359 5999

There are several branches of this welcoming restaurant, which is particularly good for children as they have a

Antiques and bric à brac are on offer at Camden Passage

special kids' menu and a no-smoking policy. The food is 'fusion': Latin American, Mediterranean, North African. A great brunch is available. **££–£££**

✕ Lola's
The Mall Building,
359 Upper Street, N1
Tube: Angel
Telephone: 020 7359 1932

Situated in a converted tram shed, eating here is a fairly unique experience. Modern European food of the highest quality is joined by a superb wine list. 'Wine flights' are available, where you can take the opportunity to taste five wines and then order the one you liked best. **£££–££££**

✕ Gallipoli
102 Upper Street, N1
Tube: Angel
Telephone: 020 7359 0630

It's the cosy, buzzing Turkish atmosphere that sells this place, with great authentic dishes to match. If this one's busy, try their other branch at 120 Upper Street. **££**

✕ Afghan Kitchen
35 Islington Green, N1
Tube: Angel
Telephone: 020 7359 8019

This unique eatery is one of Islington's most well-reviewed restaurants. It serves cheap and cheerful Afghan food for those who are inspired to try something a little different. **££**

Covent Garden Apple and Jubilee Markets
www.coventgardenmarket.co.uk
Covent Garden, WC2
Tube: Covent Garden
Hours: Apple Market: 10am–7pm Tuesday –Sunday;
Jubilee Market Hall: 6am–4pm Monday
Free admission

In the centre of the square designed by Inigo Jones in 1631 are market buildings that were built between 1828 and 1831. Until 1974, these buildings housed London's principal market for fruit and vegetables. When the market moved to another location, the buildings were refurbished and now feature shops, restaurants, cafés and pubs, as well as these markets, which offer some interesting and fun shopping adventures. The Apple Market sells arts and crafts, pottery, silverware, clothes and jewellery. The Jubilee Market Hall sells mostly antiques but also some newer items and reproductions.

✕ **For dining options, please see Covent Garden on pages 46–51 .**

Kensington Church Street
From Notting Hill to Kensington High Street, W8
Tube: Notting Hill Gate, Kensington High Street
Hours: Normal shopping hours
Free admission

Walking from the top of Kensington Church Street (at Notting Hill) towards Kensington High Street, you will be rewarded with a variety of excellent places to eat as well as some of the best up-market antiques shopping in London. Shops line both sides of the street, so take care when criss-crossing from one to another.

✕ Clarke's

www.sallyclarke.com
124 Kensington Church Street, W8
Tube: Notting Hill Gate,
Kensington High Street
Telephone: 020 7221 9225

Sally Clarke is a contemporary of Alice Waters and shares the famous Chez Panisse chef's adherence to 'fresh-fresh-fresh'. Her restaurant is a no-choice lunch or dinner that is based on whatever is in season and available that day. You can phone for the day's menu for lunch or dinner, but most diners rely on her excellence and book a table without regard to what will be served. The dining room is small, serene and lovely, and you will be captivated by the service, food and friendliness. California wines are featured. Lunch is, of course, less expensive than dinner. Reservations advised.
£££–£££££

Adjoining the restaurant is her bakery and café (**£**), which, though tiny, holds a wonderful selection of breads, pastries, cheeses and condiments, as well as a few tables in the rear where you can enjoy a coffee and pastry.

Note: Clarke's is an easy walk from **Kensington Palace**.

✕ Churchill Arms

119 Kensington Church Street, W8
Tube: Notting Hill Gate,
Kensington High Street
Telephone: 020 7792 1246

The quality of the food (Thai is the speciality but regular pub fare is also served) and ale belie the ordinary-looking pub atmosphere and there is a wide choice of excellent dishes in generous portions. The food is great value and the pub can get very crowded as a result. There is a 'garden' room in the rear and during peak times it can get smoky. **£–££**

✕ Ffiona's

51 Kensington Church Street, W8
Tube: Notting Hill Gate,
Kensington High Street
Telephone: 020 7937 4152

Ffiona's (owned by Ffiona Reid-Owen) is a homely, popular bistro where you can enjoy good food at reasonable prices. British home cooking is the speciality; a three-course meal ordered before 7.30pm is particularly good value. Locals worry that Ffiona's will become too popular, so work on your plummy accent and act like you live up the street. **££–£££**

✕ Maggie Jones

6 Old Court Place, W8
Tube: Kensington High Street
Telephone: 020 7937 6462

I don't know what the critics say, but this is one of our very favourite London restaurants. We've been coming here for over 30 years, and our children remember it from their childhood. My husband Bob and I celebrate special occasions here. We love the food, the ambience (old-fashioned English farmhouse) and the fact that it was named after Princess Margaret when she married Anthony Armstrong Jones.

The furniture is plain pine and rustic with candles stuck into bottles, the clientèle is spiffy and the food is just wonderful. Your wine will be brought to the table in a magnum, and you will be charged according to how much you drink. Standards include Stilton soufflé and Maggie's famous fish pie. Children with picky appetites might baulk at the 'different' food served here. **£££–££££**

Portobello Road
www.portobelloroad.co.uk
Portobello Road, W11
Tube: Notting Hill Gate, Ladbroke Grove
Hours: 9am–5pm Saturdays (dealers arrive before 6am)
Free admission

Some shops open during the week, and the vegetable and flower market is open daily except Mondays, but Saturday is the big day. Since this is such a well-known market and so popular, try to arrive ahead of the throng (8.30–9am). The narrow street gets jam-packed with people and stalls – a real crush in high season.

The south end is antiques and some reproductions, merging into the fruit, vegetable and flower carts, then as you come to the overhead bridge the mood swings to funk and there will be more clothes and music than antiques (though you can still find them here and there).

If you keep going for another block or two, you will arrive at Golborne Road. If you bear right, you will find yourself in another atmosphere entirely, mainly Moroccan, Turkish and Middle Eastern, with the appropriate food shops and spices. On Friday and Saturday they also set up street stalls for antiques and junk.

✕ EATING AROUND PORTOBELLO ROAD

I will begin at Notting Hill Gate tube at the corner of Notting Hill Gate and Pembridge Road, which will lead you to Portobello Road. Once you are on Portobello Road (which begins when you cross Chepstow Villas) there will be many cafés to choose from as well as the famous **Earl of Lonsdale** pub, 277–281 Westbourne Grove, which serves good food. I've started with a breakfast stop.

✕ Manzara

24 Pembridge Road, W11
Tube: Notting Hill Gate
Telephone: 020 7727 3062

From the tube, this is one of the first places you will pass en route to Portobello. It is wonderful, and it is worth making an early start just for the excuse to stop here for a cappuccino and an almond croissant. Their full menu, featuring Greek salads, hot savoury pastries, kebabs and pastries, is not available during Saturday market hours because of the crowds, but is available later in the day and, of course, at other times during the week. **£**

✕ **Osteria Basilico**

29 Kensington Park Road, W11
Tube: Notting Hill Gate
Telephone: 020 7727 9957

The authentic Italian Osteria Basilico serves exceptionally good homemade dishes including pasta and pizzas, meat, fish and salads. The service is friendly and the ambience is lovely.

It's so popular though that for lunch on Saturdays you must arrive just before 12.30pm to get a table. Otherwise, wait until the first wave of diners has left then return. It will be worth it. This is also a very popular evening spot. **££–£££**

✄ Café Med Bar and Grill

184 Kensington Park Road, W11
Tube: Notting Hill Gate
Telephone: 020 7221 1150

I like this café for its ambience and friendly service. The food is reasonably priced and there are plenty of out-of-the-ordinary Mediterranean dishes. The small cover charge includes delicious Pugliese bread with marinated olives and aromatic oil. **£££**

✄ Felicitous

19 Kensington Park Road, W11
Tube: Notting Hill Gate
Telephone: 020 1243 4050

A bright yellow awning shelters the few outside tables, and the glass windows showcase the gourmet food and groceries inside. They do a strong catering business here, and the glass cases are jammed with a diverse selection of meats, fish, vegetables and salads. This is a one-stop

Portobello Road in west London has something for everyone

place to order food to take away and to buy food-related gifts, hampers and baskets, wines, cheeses, chocolates and breads. After you have scanned everything in this small shop you'll be ready for a little treat yourself. Bliss. **£–££**

✕ Mediterraneo

37 Kensington Park Road, W11
Tube: Notting Hill Gate
Telephone: 020 7792 3131

This is a sister to Osteria Basilico (see page 78) and another good choice (though not quite as enjoyable). They have good fish and vegetarian dishes as well as other Italian favourites. You are advised to book. **££–£££**

✕ Books For Cooks

www.booksforcooks.com
4 Blenheim Crescent, W11
Tube: Ladbroke Grove, Notting Hill Gate, Westbourne Park
Telephone: 020 7221 1992

A short walk to your left off Portobello will bring you to this well-known bookshop with a tiny kitchen in the rear and a few tables set up. You can buy whatever the guest chef has made that day and be confident that it will be delicious. Carrot, ginger and honey soup, for example, was the perfect antidote to the chilly weather outside one day. There will usually be a luncheon casserole or salad and several sweets. It's never the same from one day to the next, and the chef often has a new book out that he/she will sign for you. In nice weather more tables are set up outside; there are also sofas for book browsing inside. **£–££**

✕ Argile Gallery & Café

7 Blenheim Crescent, W11
Tube: Ladbroke Grove, Notting Hill Gate, Westbourne Park
Telephone: 020 7792 0888

Across the street from Books For Cooks, the Argile serves nice sandwiches, soups and small main courses. All the art on the walls is for sale. **£–££**

✕ EATING FURTHER DOWN PORTOBELLO ROAD

The general rule is the farther down Portobello Road you go, the cheaper it gets. Underneath the Westway Flyover on the right are several cafés serving good food at budget prices.

✕ Makan

Portobello Road, W10
Tube: Ladbroke Grove
Telephone: 020 8960 5169

Serves authentic Malay food to eat in or take away. Very good and very popular. **£**

✕ Sausage and Mash

Portobello Road, W10
Tube: Ladbroke Grove
Telephone: 020 8968 8898

This café is better than it sounds. They serve a variety of bangers with mash, as well as salads and desserts. **£**

✕ Brasserie du Marché aux Puces

349 Portobello Road, W10
Tube: Ladbroke Grove
Telephone: 020 8968 5828

This is a good place to eat if you passed up on some of the above cafés and restaurants. They serve a light breakfast and the set-price lunch is good value (sirloin of beef with béarnaise sauce followed by crème brûlée). They also serve a weekend brunch and a three-course Sunday lunch. The atmosphere is simple and rustic, but this corner café is somewhat pricey. **££–£££**

✕ EATING AROUND GOLBORNE ROAD

If you are still in the mood to search for something unique to look at or buy, keep going past the really downbeat junk until you come to Golborne Road, then turn right. On Fridays and Saturdays there will be carts along the pavement with various offerings.

✕ Café Oporto

62A Golborne Road, W10
Tube: Ladbroke Grove
Telephone: 020 8968 8839

Oporto has wonderful take-away and eat-in items behind the glass counter, with unusual sandwich fillings. This place is extremely popular. Open 8am–8pm every day. **£**

✕ Lisboa Patisserie

57 Golborne Road, W10
Tube: Ladbroke Grove
Telephone: 020 8968 5242

Oporto's rival, this cafe is similarly popular and is jam-packed most mornings and overflowing on Saturdays because the pastries and fresh cappuccinos are wonderful. The custard tarts are outstanding. Open 8am to 8pm every day. **£**

MUSEUMS AND LIBRARIES

The museums and libraries of London display collections of the greatest artefacts and achievements, certainly giving food for thought to all who gaze upon these wonders of the creative and investigative mind.

The arresting statue of Sir Isaac Newton in the Grand Piazza of the British Library is the work of Edouard Paolozzi.

The museum, built in 1753, has had a facelift and the new Great Court, designed by Britain's leading architect, Sir Norman Foster, is simply stunning. Located in the centre of the museum, straight ahead as you enter, your first impression is of light, space and grandeur. Marbled floors and creamy ivory walls reflect the natural daylight pouring in through the soaring glass ceiling. Twin staircases that rise from either side of the centre core lead you up to the Court Restaurant. The ground floor holds exhibition space, gift shops and bookshops (including one especially for young people) and two coffee and snack points.

The British Museum is reputed to be one of the greatest museums in the world, with exhibits showing the works of man from prehistory to the present. Your first visit should include the exquisite pre-Christian Portland Vase, the Rosetta Stone, the Black Obelisk, the Elgin Marbles and the ever-popular Egyptian royal tombs and mummies. The experience of seeing this vast collection of treasures is impressive; however, there is so much you can overdose in one visit. You simply cannot view it entirely in a single day, but since admission is free (though a donation is appreciated), and so long as time allows, you can make a series of visits. If you are making repeat visits, you get the chance to try out a number of eating options both within the museum and nearby.

The museum is located in scholarly Bloomsbury with its wonderful literary history, today a mix of university students and office workers in an atmosphere of beautiful Georgian squares and architecture. Former residents of the neighbourhood, such as novelists Virginia Woolf (1882–1941) and E.M. Forster (1879–1970), would find the area much the same today.

✗ EATING IN THE BRITISH MUSEUM

The **Court Restaurant** opens daily at 11am, with last orders at 5.30pm Sunday–Wednesday, and at 9pm Thursday–Saturday. Lunch is served 12 noon–3.30pm. Afternoon Tea is available 3.30–5.30pm; dinner is served 5.30–9pm Thursday to Saturday.

Main courses could include chicken casserole with Norfolk dumplings or a wild mushroom tart with new potatoes and mixed salad. For dessert, perhaps a mango and papaya fruit brûlée or smoked red Leicester cheese with pear jam. Children's portions are available. Also popular is the Bento box, inspired by the Aomori Float and Japanese Kites in the Wellcome Gallery. Items are often featured on the menu to tie in with temporary exhibitions. **££–£££**

The British Museum holds some of the world's finest antiquities

In the Great Court are two **snack areas** with long steel tables and benches. It's almost like eating outdoors as you can see the sky and clouds through the glass roof overhead. **£**

Located on the main floor is the **Gallery Café**, a Milburn restaurant as found in some of the other major museums in London and beyond. This is cafeteria-style with a great variety of choice, including wine, and the dining area has frescos and high windows. **£–££**

✕ Le Bistro Savoir Faire

42 New Oxford Street, WC1
Tube: Tottenham Court Road
Telephone: 020 7436 0707

This bistro is inexpensive and serves very good fare with daily changing specials. The décor is rather 'Moulin Rouge' and the tables and chairs are rustic and

unmatched. The bistro is famous for its good value, high-quality, two-course lunch. Evening prices rise slightly but are still reasonable. **££**

✕ Pizza Express

30 Coptic Street, WC1
Tube: Tottenham Court Road
Telephone: 020 7636 3232

This is another location for this very good chain. You will go past it if you are walking towards the bistro described above (and may well stop here instead of continuing). This particular branch of Pizza Express was the first in the chain and opened in 1965, and it is generally acknowledged to be one of the best in terms of ambience and décor. The history of the building in which it is sited carries over to the restaurant, giving you an especially warm and comfortable atmosphere. **££**

✕ Coffee Gallery

23 Museum Street, WC1
Tube: Tottenham Court Road
Telephone: 020 7436 0455

This small café serves delicious Italian sandwiches and hot dishes at lunchtime and is often quite crowded. **£**

✕ Pancake Café

28 Museum Street, WC1
Tube: Tottenham Court Road
Telephone: 020 7636 2383

Sweet and savoury pancakes, many vegetarian options, plus all-day breakfasts, bagels and salads. The melts and falafel are particularly delicious. **££**

British Library

www.bl.uk
96 Euston Road, NW1
Tube: King's Cross, Euston
Telephone: 020 7412 7332
Hours: 9.30am–6pm Monday, Wednesday–Friday; 9.30am–8pm Tuesday; 9.30am–5pm Saturday; 11am–5pm Sunday
Free admission

The British Library is funded by the government to be the custodian of the most important research collection in the world,with material spanning almost 3,000 years and originating from every continent. You will find Magna Carta, the Gutenberg Bibles, the First Folio Shakespeare, Leonardo da Vinci's Notebook and the earliest, dated, printed book – *Diamond Sutra*.

As well as housing millions of books (the basement alone has shelving for 12 million volumes) the library also provides a magnificent setting for a number of major works of art, most of which hang in the library's public areas. The King's Library, which holds 65,000 volumes of the collection of George III, is a six-storey glass-walled tower at the heart of the building. All who use the restaurant and café can enjoy its beauty and its operation as a working library.

This new ultra-modern and elegant building is the largest public building to have been constructed in the United Kingdom in the entire 20th century. It boasts a piazza, three exhibition galleries, bookshop, café, restaurant, public events programme and tours.

✕ EATING AT THE BRITISH LIBRARY

The cafeteria-style **British Library Café** on level 1 offers cakes, pastries and other morning treats with coffees and teas. A daily-changing lunch menu, plus soups, salads, sandwiches and filled bagels, is available 12 noon–3pm. The dining tables overlook the King's Library. **£**

On the next level is the larger, cafeteria-style **British Library Food Hall**. The dining booths and tables are set under a soaring skylight and also overlook the King's Library. A wide selection of hot and cold dishes with vegetarian options is available all day. Full English breakfasts are a speciality and the à la carte breakfasts are also good. At lunchtime a deli bar is featured, as well as jacket potatoes with many toppings to choose from. **£**

✕ EATING ON THE EUSTON ROAD

On Euston Road at the street entrance to the library is the tiny **Chapter Coffee Shop** selling coffees, teas, fizzy drinks, juices and pastries. **£**

Across from the British Library you will find **Starbucks** and **Pizza Express,** plus a popular pub called the **Euston Flyer**. All serve meals throughout the day.

Imperial War Museum

www.iwm.org.uk
Lambeth Road, SE1
Tube: Lambeth North,
Waterloo, Southwark,
Elephant & Castle
Telephone: 020 7416 5320
Hours: 10am–6pm
Free admission

A visit to the Imperial War Museum, often overlooked by tourists, is rewarding for both adults and children. Histories of all the major world wars are depicted in hands-on exhibits, real tanks, submarines, weapons and aircraft and themed areas that provide an in-depth and sympathetic vision of battles fought, won and lost.

The museum offers personal insights of war– some may well bring a lump to your throat – which bring life and meaning to what we usually only read about or watch on television. You can experience the Blitz, enter a trench from World War I with authentic smells and sounds, listen to actual radio broadcasts made during the Battle of Britain and even try on the kit of a World War I soldier. There are also exhibitions on wars fought across the world, including the Korean War. The ground-floor display of military vehicles, rockets, artillery and planes suspended from the ceiling are always a hit with children. Also, there is a typical World War II home complete with the furniture, food and literature of that period, including the toys.

The top floor is devoted to the Holocaust, which is intensely emotional viewing. Older children, especially those who have read Anne Frank, will be able to understand the exhibit, but I do not recommend it for youngsters under eight.

The gift shop on the ground floor is a treasure trove for young people and the wonderful book section is good for everyone. Beyond the café in the museum itself, which is very good, there are not a lot of other food options nearby.

The Spitfire fighter plane can be examined up-close in the Imperial War Museum

✂ EATING IN THE IMPERIAL WAR MUSEUM

Located to the left on the main floor, the **café** is open for teas 10am–12 noon and 3–5.30pm, and for lunch 12 noon–3pm.

Service is cafeteria-style and everything is freshly prepared and delicious. A children's lunchbox is available. Being under the culinary umbrella of Milburns, the quality is, as usual, very high. **£–££**

London Transport Museum
www.ltmuseum.co.uk
Covent Garden Piazza, WC2
Telephone: 020 7379 6344
Tube: Covent Garden
Hours: 10am–6pm (opens at 11am on Fridays); closed 24–26 December
Admission charge

The museum is located to your left as you face the Jubilee Market (see page 74) in the piazza in the heart of Covent Garden. If you think the tube isn't very interesting, a visit here should change your mind. Browse the wonderful gift shop, at least, before deciding if you wish to pay a small fee to enter the museum beyond, which offers a spectacular collection of vehicles, such as buses, trams and tube trains, with working exhibits plus 15 Kidzones: interactive areas for children. It is lively and colourful and children love it.

The museum shop is well stocked, and the London Underground (tube) posters for sale are especially good and are close to being fine art. They are highly original, make interesting wall hangings, and are for sale in various sizes.

✕ As the London Transport Museum is in Covent Garden, please see pages 46–51 for dining options.

Museum of London

www.museumoflondon.org.uk
London Wall, EC2
Tube: St Paul's, Barbican, Moorgate
Telephone: 020 7600 0807
Hours: 10am–5.50pm Monday–Saturday; 12 noon–5.50pm Sunday
Free admission

The entire museum is devoted to London. Heathrow airport, for example, was once home to dinosaurs and it is fascinating to stand before a large movie screen and watch the site fade from Tyrannosaurus Rex to Concorde taking off. The story of London is followed in open galleries arranged in chronological order. Particularly charming is a recreated Victorian shop area. Other attractions include the Great Fire Experience and a display of Elizabethan jewellery.

If you are visiting the Barbican during the day, it is a good idea to include the Museum of London in your sightseeing. Simply follow the yellow lines that lead you to the museum via an array of shops and cafés under cover and over the London Wall. The distance between the two on the Highwalk is about a 5-minute stroll. And once you have toured the Museum of London, it's not far to St Paul's Cathedral. Or you can reverse the plan, ending up at the Barbican and staying on for a performance.

✕ EATING AT THE MUSEUM OF LONDON

The **Museum of London** Café is run by the caterers 'digby trout'. Hours are 10am–5pm Monday–Saturday and 11.30am–5.50pm Sunday. **£–££**

✕ As the Museum of London is near the Barbican Centre, please see pages 45–46 for further dining options.

Natural History Museum

www.nhm.ac.uk
Cromwell Road, SW7
Tube: South Kensington
Telephone: 020 7492 5011
Hours: Monday–Saturday 10am–6pm, Sunday and Bank holidays 11am–6pm
Free admission

Here is the world's leading museum of natural history, inspiring to adults, awesome to children. Situated in one of London's finest Gothic Revival buildings, the hundreds of exciting interactive experiences include exploring phenomena such as

The dinosaur exhibition is probably the most popular attraction in the Natural History Museum

earthquakes, volcanoes and tornadoes in the Earth Galleries, and viewing spectacular dinosaur habitats, rainforests and more. The bug and butterfly gallery is amazing. Note that many school groups visit the museum. If you see a group, it might be better if you make a temporary detour, as the children can be very noisy.

✖ EATING AT THE NATURAL HISTORY MUSEUM

There are four eating options within the Natural History Museum.

Hot and cold food is available at the family-oriented **Life Galleries** **Restaurant** and at the childrens' favourite **Globe Fast Food**.

Drinks and snacks are available from the **Waterhouse Café** and the **Snack Bar and Picnic Area**, where you can also eat your own sandwiches. **£–££**

✖ For dining options beyond the Natural History Museum, please see pages 94–95.

Science Museum
www.sciencemuseum.org.uk
Exhibition Road, SW7
Tube: South Kensington
Telephone: 0870 870 4771
Hours: 10am–6pm; closed 24–26 December
Free admission, except for special exhibitions

There are five floors of wonder in this fantastic museum, which is a favourite of everyone. All ages love it here: adults like the hands-on galleries as much as children do. From flight to chemicals to trains and ships, from docks and diving to health, heat and 'food for thought' – the array of displays and exhibitions is stunning in its diversity and appeal. An IMAX cinema shows spectacular 2-D and 3-D films accompanied by stereo sound on a screen as high as five double-decker buses. There are plenty of interactive exhibits to enliven the interest of the most tired child, or adult for that matter. You will hardly be able to tear yourselves away to eat.

⚔ EATING AT THE SCIENCE MUSEUM

Long tables underlit with blue neon set the atmosphere in the **Deep Blue Café** that is housed in an open-plan, waiter-service restaurant on the ground floor. Excellent fresh and delicious food, plus hot and cold drinks, beer and wine, are served in an interesting atmosphere. **£–££**

The small cafeteria-style **Museum Café** on the ground floor has a selection of hot and cold drinks, sandwiches, soup and pastries; hot meals are served 12 noon–3pm. There is a roped-off eating area which adjoins the concourse. **£**

The **Eat Drink Shop** in the basement and the **Gallery Cafe** on the third floor both serve hot and cold snacks and drinks. **£**

⚔ For dining options beyond the Science Museum, please see pages 94–95.

Victoria and Albert Museum

www.vam.ac.uk
Exhibition Road, SW7
Tube: South Kensington
Telephone: 020 7942 2000 (main switchboard), 0870 442 0808 (general information)
Hours: 10am–5.45pm, except Wednesdays and the last Friday of the month when the museum is open until 10pm; closed 24–25 December
Free admission, except for special exhibitions

This and the British Museum are the two must-see museums of London if your time is short. The 146 galleries display art from cultures around the world. Collections date from 3000 BC to the present with occasional special exhibitions. Exhibits include sculpture, jewellery, photographs, glass, ceramics and silver, furniture, textiles and antiquities. The gift shop is large and sells not only copies of many of the exhibits but also costume jewellery, small toys, books, and an enormous selection of greeting cards and stationery. This is a terrific place to do your souvenir shopping. Children can explore the collections from the activity carts or by taking a backpack tour.

⚔ EATING AT THE VICTORIA AND ALBERT MUSEUM

The New Restaurant is open until 5.30pm (9pm on Wednesdays). If you are planning to take an extensive tour of the museum, this is the place to take a break. Prices are inexpensive, the food is excellent, and the atmosphere is pleasant. Live jazz or classical music is performed on some Wednesdays and Sundays to accompany your meal. **££**

The outdoor Pirelli Garden is open for picnics during fine weather and also offers a pleasant green space to sit and relax or let your children play safely. Entrance is only from within the museum.

⚔ Greenfield's
13 Exhibition Road, SW7
Tube: South Kensington
Telephone: 020 7584 1396

This busy café is between South Kensington tube and the Victoria and Albert Museum. There is a scattering of tables inside with more spilling out onto the pavement during nice weather. You'll find plenty of options here, and you can eat in or take away (to enjoy, for example, on the patio outside the Natural History Museum). **£**

⚔ Oriental Canteen
2a Exhibition Road, SW7
Tube: South Kensington
Telephone: 020 7581 8831

The dozen or so counter-high tables seem always to be full, but service is quick and the wait is never long. The rice and noodle combinations on the long menu are particularly good value. Pork, duck, chicken, beef and prawns, as well as vegetables, are prepared many different ways. Choose from Tiger beer, juice or fizzy drinks to wash it down. **£**

⚔ Crêperie de Hampstead
2a Exhibition Road, SW7
Tube: South Kensington
Telephone: 020 7589 8947

Next door to the Oriental Canteen is this Crêperie. Delicious crêpes are filled with imaginative sweet fillings – you can even choose your chocolate (milk, dark, white Belgian or chocolate syrup). Banana Maple Cream Dream is their most popular creation and has been so for more than 20 years. There are savoury crêpes, too, including plenty of good vegetarian options. And as well as regular crêpes there are nutty buckwheat-flour Breton galettes. **££**

✕ Polish Club/Restaurant

55 Princes Gate, SW7
Tube: South Kensington
Telephone: 020 7589 4635

I debated whether to include this find in the book, as it is actually a private club. But when I explained to the friendly people inside what I was doing, they assured me it was fine to mention them here. The location, just yards from the great museums in this area and almost opposite the Science Museum, is perfect not only for lunch or dinner, but also just for coffee or a drink while you take a break, either mid-morning or mid-afternoon. Entering from the street you will think you are in a small, quietly elegant hotel. But walk in and to your left you will find a beautiful bar area with comfortable chairs, small tables and floor-to-ceiling windows. The small dining room beyond is bright and cheerful and looks out to a lovely green park. The menu is not large and the focus is, of course, on Polish

food. Prices are slightly higher for non-members, but still very reasonable given the wonderful setting. **££–£££**

✕ Joe's

126 Draycott Avenue, SW3
Tube: South Kensington
Telephone: 020 7225 2217

Across from the Coco Chanel boutique and near the wonderful Michelin building you will find Joe's, right next to Joseph Clothing Shop (restaurant and shop both owned by fashion designer Joseph Ettedgui). Other branches of the restaurant can be found in Sloane Street and Fenwicks Department Store, Regent Street.

This is a trendy area and a fun place to window-shop. The restaurant is glamorous and is often filled with celebrities. The food is described as modern European. The starters are interesting and it's fine to make a meal of them and skip the main course if you're on a diet or a budget. Tables for quick meals are near the front, and a few steps up is the more leisurely dining area. Brunch is served Sunday, which is the cheapest way to enjoy Joe's. Reservations recommended. **££–£££**

PARKS AND GARDENS

London is fortunate enough to have acres of green space scattered throughout the city. The smallest glint of sunshine will inspire an outing to a park or garden, and a hot, sunny day will find every deck chair occupied. An ice-cream cone from a park kiosk could make your stroll that much more rich and satisfying.

The Chinese Pagoda in Kew Gardens was built as a surprise for Princess Augusta in 1761.

Green Park and St James's Park

www.royalparks.gov.uk/james
www.royalparks.gov.uk/green
Tubes: Green Park, St James's Park, Victoria,
Westminster, Charing Cross, Hyde Park Corner
Telephone: 020 7930 1793
Free admission

These two landscaped beauties form an almost unbroken chain. St James's is a popular picnic area featuring a lovely lake stocked with ducks and pelicans, with deckchairs to hire, and as it is adjacent to Buckingham Palace it is considered the most royal of London's royal parks. If possible, travel to the parks via Westminster tube station, a newly renovated marvel of steel and 21st-century engineering. Leave the station via exit 6. At the top of the stairs, look up and be thrilled by the stunning sight before you: Big Ben, Westminster Abbey and the spires of Parliament.

Walk down Great George Street, away from Big Ben, bear right on Horse Guards Road, pass the Cabinet War Rooms (open to the public), continue to the Horse Guards Parade and opposite is an entrance to St James's Park. (The walk takes only a few minutes.) Walk left to pass St James's Palace and Clarence House and into Green Park. You will see the Victoria Memorial facing Buckingham Palace. If you see the flag flying over the palace it means the queen is in residence.

✕ EATING IN ST JAMES'S PARK

The Cake House is located near the entrance to St James's Park at Horse Guards Road. You can pick up a snack to take out to the picnic benches or to sit on the lawn.

You may be there when the resident pelican is standing by for treats and photo shoots.

There is a **refreshment kiosk** near the children's playground for sandwiches, snacks, sweets and drinks. **£**

There are no cafés in Green Park.

✕ For dining options beyond the parks, please see the listings for Westminster Abbey on pages 31–33 for the south-west end of St James's Park, Piccadilly on pages 113–115 for the north end of Green Park and Buckingham Palace on pages 25–28.

Holland Park sits in a leafy residential area, a haven for the occupants of the elegant surrounding townhouses. The strutting peacocks delight children and there is also a small playground. Less formal than Hyde Park, it has a wonderful natural charm.

✕ EATING IN HOLLAND PARK

There are picnic tables and **snack bars** as well as a little **café** within the park. The café is well signposted and serves soups, sandwiches and snacks. New management has promised to keep prices low. **£**

✕ Julie's Bar

www.juliesrestaurant.com
135 Portland Road, W11
Tube: Holland Park
Telephone: 020 7229 8331

Julie's is special. It's one of those places that you want to instantly claim as your favourite. Entering into a cosy bar, you will find the atmosphere of the Raj captivating, and your first moments will be spent just taking in the interior. The rooms meander charmingly and a mahogany staircase leads you upstairs to three more intimate dining areas, another small bar and a continuation of the charming décor. The blend of Indian and British styles results in a quirky and utterly delightful setting. The food is British, but updated to reflect the evolving culinary scene in London. The menu changes seasonally and includes good-value daily specials. **££–£££**

Next door to Julie's Bar is Julie's Restaurant. The menu is British, up-market and more expensive, but also excellent. **££££**

✕ Maison Blanc

www.maisonblanc.co.uk
102 Holland Park Avenue, W11
Tube: Holland Park
Telephone: 020 7221 2494

The original branch of the French patisserie where you can be assured of getting authentic croissants. See also pages 59 & 140. **£**

Hyde Park

www.royalparks.gov.uk/hyde
Tube: Marble Arch, Lancaster Gate, Hyde Park Corner,
Knightsbridge
Telephone: 020 7298 2100
Free admission

Perhaps the most well known of London's many parks, Hyde Park was formerly a royal hunting ground (King Henry VIII used it for deer-hunting), a site of duels and executions and it also served as a huge potato field during World War II. Today, it is simply beautiful, and a source of pleasure to everyone. Counting the adjacent Kensington Gardens, it covers an enormous 615 acres smack in the middle of London – an oasis of richly green lawns, mature trees, park benches, flowerbeds, fountains and ponds, and the wonderful 41-acre Serpentine lake which is popular for rowing, sailing model boats, and, for some, swimming (it is cold). On a sunny day it is a popular pastime to sit on one on the benches surrounding the Italian Gardens at Lancaster Gate – with an ice cream from the nearby vendor.

 EATING IN HYDE PARK

The two cafés in Hyde Park are both on the banks of the Serpentine lake. There is one on the south side, **The Lido** (020 7706 7098), and the other, **The Dell Restaurant** (020 7706 0464), is on the lake's east end. Both serve drinks and snacks. **£–££,**

The ornate bridge over the Serpentine in Hyde Park

※ For dining options beyond Hyde Park, please see the listings for Harrods and Harvey Nichols on pages 119–123 for the south end of the park and Speaker's Corner on page 69 for the north-west corner of the park.

※ The Mitre

24 Craven Terrace, W2
Tube: Lancaster Gate, Paddington
Telephone: 020 7262 5240

Good pub fare and daily specials feature here, and young people are welcome, too. We especially like the bangers and mash and the vegetarian casserole. A new chef has raised the quality and presentation of the food. There is also a ghost in the Vaults Bar on the lower ground floor. £–££

※ Taormina

19 Craven Terrace, W2
Tube: Lancaster Gate, Paddington
Telephone: 020 7262 2090

We have never had a bad meal in this popular and charming restaurant. The Spaghetti Carbonara is fantastic. They offer good service, a varied menu, starched table linens and a good house wine. Eat well here for a moderate price. ££
     Note: Next door but one is the Craven Gallery where Annie sells lovely antiques, specializing in silver and items of French provenance (she is French). She seems to have a little of everything, plus a huge warehouse of furniture nearby that she will be happy to show you. Taormina is owned by her son, so if the shop is closed ask for Annie in the restaurant.

※ Concordia

www.italiancuisine.co.uk
29–31 Craven Road, W2
Tube: Lancaster Gate, Paddington
Telephone: 020 7723 3725

Expect authentic Italian food, a warm and charming setting and generous servings. Side salads, in particular, are large enough to share. Downstairs (Concordia Notte) is a dining and cocktail bar area with dancing to live music. ££–£££

※ Mr Frascati's

34 Spring Street, W2
Tube: Paddington
Telephone: 020 7723 0319

This expensive Italian bistro serves delicious food in an intimate dining room. £££

✕ Bruno's

Craven Road, W2
Tube: Paddington

This is just a tiny sandwich shop, but I wish we had one like it in Las Vegas. Choose from great pasta, luscious, fresh sandwich fillings and all manner of breads and baguettes and a good value all-day breakfast. £

✕ Triana

9 Craven Road, W2
Tube: Paddington
Telephone: 020 7723 2063

Next door to Bruno's and boasting a talented chef, Triana is a favourite choice for consistently good Spanish food. The atmosphere is cosy and cheerful and the staff is welcoming. Everyone comes here – local residents and tourists alike.

Triana is our first dinner stop on arrival in London. The servings are generous, the service friendly and the food above average. They have some terrific daily specials. The house wine is good. ££

Kensington Gardens
www.royalparks.gov.uk/kensington
Tube: High Street Kensington, Queensway,
Lancaster Gate
Telephone: 020 7298 2100
Free admission

Hyde Park runs smoothly into Kensington Gardens. In times past, Kensington Gardens were the grounds to Kensington Palace, formerly the home of Princess Diana. There is a Diana, Princess of Wales Memorial playground in her honour. Other elements of the park include the famous Peter Pan statue, the opulent Albert Memorial and the Serpentine Gallery (020 7298 1515), where art exhibitions are held for free.

✕ EATING IN KENSINGTON GARDENS

Mentioned in the Kensington Palace description is **The** **Orangery** (page 27), the perfect place for a lunch or tea break. Snacks and drinks are also available from the **Kensington Playground**

Café (020 7727 9578), the **Albert Memorial** and the **Italian Fountain Gardens**. **£–££**

A short walk away is the Queensway area, a street teeming with shops, restaurants, cafés and the large Whiteley's Shopping Centre. See also the listings around Kensington Church Street, pages 75–76.

✕ Royal China

13 Queensway, W2
Tube: Queensway, Bayswater
Telephone: 020 7221 2535

Known for excellent dim sum that is available daily until 5.30pm, and some of the best Chinese food in London. This restaurant is consistently busy because it is very good. **££–£££**

✕ Hung Tao

51 Queensway, W2
Tube: Queensway, Bayswater
Telephone: 020 7727 5753

This is a tiny, busy place with wonderful food that you can eat in or take out. Some dishes are prepared out in front, so you can see the cook at work before you even walk in. Unlicensed and cash only. **£–££**

✕ Pierre Péchon

www.croquembouche.co.uk
Patisserie Française,
127 Queensway, W2
Tube: Queensway, Bayswater
Telephone 020 7221 4819

Established in 1925, this is a family-owned, French patisserie/café that you are sure to return to. Go in past the glass display cases of fresh breads, pastries, cakes, tarts and fresh sandwiches, to find a small dining area. Breakfast is served until 11am. The lunch menu offers huge baked potatoes, lasagne, cannelloni and even pancakes. **£–££**

✕ Whiteley's Shopping Centre

www.whiteleys.com
Queensway, W2
Tube: Queensway, Bayswater

The top floor offers a variety of places for meals, coffees, ice creams or a fast-food fix. You can choose from Chinese, Japanese, Sushi, Mexican, Italian and French. I recommend **ASK** for Italian and **Café Rouge** for French.

The large bookshop on the second floor also has a coffee place. There is **Costa Coffee** and **Café Rapallo** for coffee and pastries on the ground floor, and tables are set out in the atrium for your convenience. **£–££**

Kew Gardens

www.kew.org
Royal Botanic Gardens, Kew, Richmond, Surrey, TW9
Tube: Kew Gardens
Telephone: 020 8332 5655
Hours: 9.30am–4.15pm, November–January;
9.30am–5.30pm, February–March; 9.30am–6.30pm
Monday–Friday and 9.30am–7.30pm weekends and holi-
days, April–August; 9.30am–6pm, September–October
Admission charge

There is so much more to the Royal Botanical Gardens at Kew than just a beautiful park; it is also an important botanical research centre. The vast expanse of lawn and formal gardens feature two 19th-century Victorian conservatories – the Princess of Wales Conservatory for tropical plants and the Palm House,

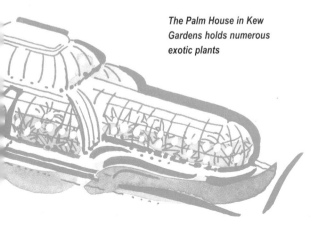

The Palm House in Kew Gardens holds numerous exotic plants

which contains exotic rainforest plant life – as well as the Temperate House and Queen Charlotte's Cottage. More than 60,000 species of plants can be found in this 300-acre area, making it a gardener's paradise. Special events ensure that there is always something interesting happening at Kew, from Japanese garden exhibits to tree-climbing demonstrations.

✕ EATING AT KEW GARDENS

Refreshments and hot and cold dishes are available from the **Pavilion Restaurant** near Temperate House. **£**

Morning coffee, lunches and waitress-service afternoon tea is available from **The Orangery** (020 8332 5157) near the Main Gate. **£–££**

At the Victoria Gate entrance is the **Visitor Centre** where you can purchase drinks and snacks. **White Peaks café** near the Farm also serves drinks and snacks. **£** The brochure shows the location of all eating areas.

✕ Brown's

3–5 Kew Green, TW9
Tube: Kew Gardens
Telephone: 020 8948 4838

Serving bistro food in lovely light and airy surroundings, this is a great place for lunch. Morning coffee and dinner are also available. **££–£££**

✕ Maids of Honour

288 Kew Road, TW9
Tube: Kew Gardens
Telephone: 020 8940 2752

Serves an à la carte menu and set teas with delicious homemade cakes. **£–££**

Regent's Park
www.royalparks.gov.uk/regent
Tube: Regent's Park, Baker Street, Great Portland Street, St John's Wood, Camden Town
Telephone: 020 7486 7905
Free admission

This beautiful park is home to the Open-air Theatre and London Zoo. Its core is a rose garden that surrounds a small lake teeming with waterfowl and spanned by Japanese bridges. Designed by John Nash in the 19th century, it is considered the jewel of

London's parks. Here, as in other parks, you can hire a deckchair for a small fee and sunbathe surrounded by the scent of roses.

✕ EATING IN REGENT'S PARK

The **Rose Garden Buffet Park Café** (020 7935 5729) is a 10-minute walk from the Boating Lake and a blaze of colour throughout spring and summer – many tables are set among the blooms. As well as hot and cold dishes and some healthy food options, there is an ice-cream parlour. **£–££**

On the Broadwalk is a Swiss-style chalet, the **Broadwalk Café** (020 7724 3872), with a large sun patio. It serves hot and cold snacks, soups and pastries. **£**

The **café** at the **Tennis Centre** (020 7486 4216) has a relaxed, clubhouse atmosphere and healthy, cosmopolitan food. It is licensed and very popular. **£–£££**

The **Boathouse Café** (020 7724 4069) serves drinks, snacks and sandwiches. **£**

✕ Patisserie Valerie at the RIBA

www.patisserie-valerie.co.uk
RIBA, 66 Portland Place, W1
Tube: Baker Street, Oxford Circus, Great Portland Street
Telephone: 020 7631 0467

South of Regent's Park, in the handsome Florence Hall of the Royal Institute of British Architects you can enjoy brunch or lunch from a delicious menu produced by this excellent, small patisserie chain. The menu boasts some terrific international-eclectic dishes. **££**

The aviary at London Zoo in Regent's Park

SHOPPING

It just doesn't matter what you like
or what you want to buy, Harrods in
Knightsbridge will have it.
But for other angles on what is cool,
hip, extravagant, charming or
desirable, check out any of the city's
other major shopping haunts.
British design is cutting edge,
so don't miss it.

The Queen of Time presides over Selfridges, but be sure to leave yourself
enough time to have a good look around this wonderful department store.

Marks and Spencer at Marble Arch
www.marksandspencers.com
458 Oxford Street, W1C
Tube: Marble Arch, Bond Street
Telephone: 020 7935 7954
Hours: 9am–9pm Monday–Friday; 8.30am–7.30pm
Saturday; 12 noon–6pm Sunday

Marks and Spencer's is the country's signature store. The flagship location on Oxford Street is the biggest and best branch of all. Even the queen buys her knickers here – so it is said. You really haven't seen England until you go into a branch of Marks and Sparks. They now have dressing rooms to try things on (which they used not to have), and they also accept credit cards (which they used not to do). Welcome to the modern age! As well as excellent value and quality clothing, they have recently introduced a more up-market designer range, Autograph, and a specialist range for the more trendy, Per Una.

✖ EATING IN MARKS AND SPENCERS, MARBLE ARCH

This enormous branch of Marks and Spencers now has two branches of the company's **Café Revive**, very appropriately named for a refreshment venue in such a huge store. These can be found in the home supplies department on the third floor and in the lower ground floor, which also holds the enormous food hall. Sandwiches, salads, cakes, pastries and coffee are available. **£**

Selfridges
www.selfridges.com
Oxford Street, W1
Tube: Marble Arch
Telephone: 0870 8377 377
Hours: 10am–8pm Monday–Friday; 9.30am–8pm
Saturday; 12 noon–6pm Sunday

The first and some say the best department store in England. Harrods usually takes the 'best' title, but Selfridges is still a terrific shopping experience. Their food hall isn't large, but it has some of the best offerings in the city and the smaller size makes it easier to navigate than the gargantuan food hall at Harrods. They seem to carry the very latest products, as well as the timelessly classic, in every department. Selfridges also has a multitude of concessions, such as Skandium in homeware and Top Shop in Selfridges Spirit, so there is no need to trawl the high street.

✕ EATING IN SELFRIDGES

Plenty of food to eat here – such as sushi at the **Yo! Sushi** bar – or take away. The international food counter is especially good. In the store itself, every floor is full of wonderful things as well as many places to stop for a meal, or just coffee or tea. The lower ground floor has a **Coffee Bar** I especially like. It's smack in the middle of the shopping so you can keep looking while you enjoy your latte. Also very good is the small self-service café on the mezzanine for tea and scones, as well as delicious light meals.

The clock above the main entrance to Selfridges

If you're with a group and you all fancy something different head for the Food Garden Café on the fifth floor, where there are a number of food counters serving food from all over the world.

Whatever your budget and taste, there is something for everyone in Selfridges. **£–£££**

✂ For dining options outside of Marks and Spencer and Selfridges, please see the listings for St Christopher's Place on pages 20–21.

Fenwicks

www.fenwick.co.uk
63 New Bond Street, W1
Tube: Bond Street
Telephone: 020 7629 9161
Hours: 10am–6.30pm Monday–Saturday (open until 8pm on Thursdays)

As you continue east along Oxford Street you will come to New Bond Street. Here is a very special department store that is worth checking out: Fenwicks. (It is pronounced 'Fennics' – leave out the 'w'.) It is tucked just behind busy Oxford Street on New Bond Street near Hanover Square. Smaller than most department stores, it is easier to navigate when you are clothes shopping. Some top designers carry their lines here. Especially charming is the hat department – where you can find both outlandish and glamorous chapeaux. The store is long established and caters more to the British than to tourists (who usually don't wander far from busy Oxford Street). The location is charming as well, with auction houses near by and a more subdued atmosphere both within the store and in the surrounding area.

✂ EATING IN FENWICKS

On the second floor is **Joe's Restaurant** (see page 95 for more details on this small chain of exclusive restaurants), packed with smartly dressed women, including those from the fashion world, and offers elegant salads as well as food with more calories.

Enjoy the bustling, chattering atmosphere. **££–£££**

New on the scene, on the lower ground floor, is **Carluccio's Caffé** (020 7629 0699). As well as delicious food, it has a well-stocked delicatessen. **£–££**

✕ Café at Sotheby's

34–35 New Bond Street, W1
Tube: Bond Street, Oxford Circus
Telephone: 020 7293 5077

Inside the famous Sotheby's Auction House is a wonderful café. Here you can enjoy lovely lunches of 'healthy' modern British dishes at a reasonable price. Especially popular is their lobster club sandwich, and their teatime menu. Into the bargain is a glimpse of the auction house, where many a Master has been bought and sold, and, perhaps, a chance to view some treasures. **££**

✕ For further dining options, please see the listings for John Lewis and Liberty on pages 110–113.

John Lewis

www.johnlewis.com
278 Oxford Street, W1A
Tube: Bond Street, Oxford Circus
Telephone: 020 7629 7711
Hours: 9.30am–7pm Monday–Saturday (open until 8pm on Thursdays)

Back on Oxford Street is this wonderful, slightly old-fashioned department store, which has a reputation for being 'never knowingly undersold', that is it challenges you to find the same item cheaper elsewhere. Here you will find beautiful home furnishings, from china to Persian carpets. There are fashions for the entire family, a stunning selection of fabrics and an excellent electrical department.

✕ EATING IN JOHN LEWIS

There are several places for refreshments within the store, but the best spot is at a window table in the third-floor restaurant (to enjoy lunch with a view). Stations here offer an all-day breakfast, desserts and coffees, crêpes, salads and sandwiches. **£–££**

✕ Carluccio's Caffé

www.carluccios.com
8 Market Place, Oxford Circus, W1
Tube: Oxford Circus
Telephone: 020 7636 2228

It might seem that Carluccio's pops up everywhere, but there are actually only 11 branches in the whole of London. It's just that the food is so wonderful here, that it would a be a crime not to include it if it is nearby. Warning: Carluccio's is addictive. **£–££**

Liberty

www.liberty.co.uk
210–220 Regent Street, W1B
Tube: Oxford Circus, Piccadilly Circus
Telephone: 020 7734 1234
Hours: Monday–Wednesday 10am–6.30pm, Thursday 10am–8pm, Friday and Saturday 10am–7pm, Sunday 12 noon–6pm

---

Liberty, in a stunning rebuilt Tudor building, defines sublime shopping. The recent refurbishment has enlarged and updated their entire shopping concept and includes Regent House – the two are linked via interior walkways. Who has not heard of Liberty prints? Here you can find the full array in their signature scarves, clothing, small goods, bedding, curtains and, of course, fabrics.

You will be charmed by their approach to the traditional and unusual in their selection of the beautiful and the exotic: treasures and antiques rarely found in department stores. They have wonderful clothing and a smashing shoe department, as well as cutting-edge furniture, home and kitchenware items.

If you know the name Mary Quant, you might want to detour here to walk down Carnaby Street, scene of her fashion craze in the 1960s. Today it is a mish-mash of souvenirs, T-shirts and off-the-wall clothing.

✕ EATING IN LIBERTY

There are lovely cafés in both the Tudor building and Regent House. These are perfect spots to enjoy a reviving lunch, snack or cappuccino while you gear up for more shopping. Or perhaps a glass of champagne …

On the second floor of Tudor House you can order hot and cold drinks including beer, wine and champagne and choose food from an all-day menu. The Tudor Tea might tempt: cream cheese and cucumber sandwiches, fruit scone with strawberry jam and clotted cream, cake and choice of tea or coffee. The Grand Tea, rather more expensive, additionally offers a glass of champagne and smoked salmon sandwiches.

The lower ground floor of Regent House has a café with a similar menu, including breakfast served until 12 noon, savouries and cakes from 10am and afternoon teas from 3pm. There are two set tea menus here too, slightly different to those above.

Restaurants open 10am–6pm, and until 7.30pm on Thursday late-night opening. **£–£££**

✕ Café Libre
22 Great Marlborough Street, W1
Tube: Oxford Circus
Telephone: 020 7437 4106

The manager, Zuzana Mills,

has made this café a beautiful spot to eat at any time of day. Breakfast is served from 8am until 12 noon (from croissants to pancakes and the full English), then lunch gets creative with wraps, many different sandwiches, unusual salads and some main courses. Desserts take up a full page on the menu, plus you can order a cream tea. There is no special children's menu, but many items will please the most fussy eater. Just round the corner from the London Palladium (see page 132), and across the street from Liberty's side entrance. **£–££**

✕ Mildred's
45 Lexington Street, W1
Tube: Oxford Circus
Telephone: 020 7494 1634

Possibly London's best, and certainly most famous, vegetarian café, this is a slight walk east from Liberty, but well worth the detour, and suitable for the following section, Regent Street to Piccadilly Circus, too.

Mildred's is loved by people with all diets, from vegan to carnivore, as their meals are both wholesome and incredibly satisfying. Try the burger and homemade fries – it can't be beaten. Delicious desserts are on offer if you have room after your main meal, but beware they are extremely filling in themselves. The drinks menu includes Belgian wheat beer, vegetarian wine and organic lemonade. **££**

Regent Street to Piccadilly Circus
Tube: Oxford Circus, Piccadilly Circus

As you walk from Oxford Street south onto Regent Street the first department store you will pass is **Dickens and Jones** (020 7734 7070) at number 224, with five floors of ladies' fashion and well worth a look. Continuing on down Regent Street towards Piccadilly Circus you'll come to a selection of shops that used to be the domain of the horse-racing set, but which have recently found their way into the mainstream: **Burberrys** (020 7734 4060) at 165 (for the famous raincoats), **Aquascutum** (020 7675 9050, www.aquascutum.co.uk), established in 1851, at 100, and **Austin Reed** (020 7534 7877, www.austinreed.co.uk) for exquisite clothing classics. At 118 is the popular **Zara** (020 7851 4300, www.zara.com), a Spanish clothing firm with the latest look at low prices.

The famous toy store of Hamleys is a children's paradise

■ Hamleys

www.hamleys.co.uk
188-196 Regent Street, W1
Tube: Piccadilly Circus
Telephone: 0870 333 2455
Hours: 10am-8pm Monday-Friday;
9.30am-8pm Saturday; 12
noon-6pm Sunday

Hamleys is possibly the greatest toy shop in the world, and whatever your age you will love it. At Christmas time the store is particularly magical, and it is a great treat for children to be able to wander through the various departments, which house everything from Barbie dolls to motorized cars for children to drive.

✕ EATING IN HAMLEYS

There is a large **snack bar** located on the lower ground floor with child-friendly pizzas, hamburgers and so on. ££

■ Lillywhites

www.lillywhites.co.uk
24-36 Lower Regent Street, SW1
Tube: Piccadilly Circus
Telephone: 0870 333 9600
Hours: 10am-8pm Monday-Friday
(open until 9pm on Thursdays);
10am-9pm Saturday; 12 noon-6pm
Sunday

Six floors of sporting goods only, famous world-wide for snooker, shooting, skiing and everything in-between. The golf section is paradise, if golf is your passion. Be prepared to spend a lot of time browsing, shopping, swinging and putting.

✕ EATING AROUND REGENT STREET AND PICCADILLY CIRCUS

When you leave Lillywhites you have a choice of turning right to Wardour Street and the many Chinese restaurants in that area, walking down Piccadilly to the places described around Hatchards (see page 116) or, if you started your shopping marathon at the Piccadilly Circus end walking up Regent Street, to the places described on pages 112–113.

✕ The Sugar Club

21 Warwick Street, W1
Tube: Oxford Circus,
Piccadilly Circus
Telephone: 020 7437 7776

Warwick Street is a small street parallel to Regent Street, on the eastern side. The menu at The Sugar Club is modern British via New

Zealand, so Pacific Rim flavours are featured here. The food is outstanding. For evening dining it is strongly recommended to book a table. **££££**

✕ **Momo**

25-27 Heddon Street, W1
Tube: Piccadilly Circus
Telephone: 020 7434 4040

Heddon Street is just a wide alley. To find it walk south down Regent Street, and between Austin Reed and Scotch House you will see a small, unnamed street; walk in, away from Regent Street, and Heddon is tucked behind. This is just a few minutes' walk from Piccadilly Circus and all the nearby shops. The main Momo restaurant is beautiful, and specializes in Mediterranean cuisine with a strong French accent; Moroccan, Algerian and Tunisian dishes are served in a North African setting that is casual, colourful and exotic.

This is a lovely place to try a tagine (the tagine is a terracotta cooking pot in which the classic Maghrebi mix of sweet and spiced fruit, vegetables and meat is slowly simmered) or couscous.

Purely French dishes are also available, a tribute to their other location in Paris. It is recommended that you book ahead, although lunchtime tables are usually available.

Their café next door lets you sample the food and ambience in an informal, fun and exotic setting at far less cost. The fragrant mint tea (just the pouring is special) and dips with artisan bread makes a special lunch. There are lots of vegetarian dishes.

All the lighting, artefacts and paintings are for sale. Seating is on tooled leather hassocks and a scattering of chairs. This is a great find. **££–£££** in the main restaurant and **£–££** for the bazaar café next door.

Fortnum and Mason

www.fortnumandmason.com
181 Piccadilly, W1
Tube: Piccadilly Circus, Green Park
Telephone: 020 7734 8040
Hours: 10am–6.30pm Monday–Saturday, 12 noon–5pm
Sunday (Food Hall and Patio Restaurant only)

Dating back to 1707, this is the world's most divinely elegant grocery store. With royal warrants (signifying that the queen makes purchases here) it is nevertheless also accessible to those of us without royal blood.

Once inside, pick up a basket and wander the ground floor among the exquisite chocolates, teas and coffees, jams, chutneys and pâtés, Scottish smoked salmon, champagne and vinegars, tinned biscuits both sweet and savoury, and other treats you can buy to enjoy later or take home to grateful friends. Take the staircase down to the lower floor to browse the fine crystal and china, and the more casual tableware and décor as well.

Upstairs are several floors of boutiques (including a fine baby department featuring Beatrix Potter creations) with ranges for the home, as well as beauty products and fashions for men and women.

✂ EATING IN FORTNUM AND MASON

In the famed, upper-floor St James's Restaurant and Tea Salon (for which booking is recommended) traditional British fare is served in suitably formal surroundings. Slightly more relaxed are the Patio Restaurant (mezzanine floor, serving light meals and lunches) and Fountain Restaurant (meals served all day in a room decorated with fantastic murals). The spiralling wooden staircases, crystal chandeliers and deep-red carpeting of Fortnum and Mason will certainly make you feel very important indeed. **££–££££**

✂ For further dining options, please see the listings on pages 114–115 and opposite.

Hatchards

www.hatchards.co.uk
187 Piccadilly, W1
Tube: Piccadilly Circus
Telephone: 020 7439 9921
Hours: Monday–Saturday 9.30am–6.30pm (opens at 10am on Tuesdays); Sunday 12 noon–6pm

Almost next to Fortnum and Mason (see page 115) is this legendary bookshop which has been on the same spot for 200 years, looking now much as it always has. Wood panelling and staircases, heavy carpeting and a wonderful selection of fine books are your pleasure here. They carry just about every book you would want, and will order a title in for you if they are out of stock. Hatchards is second to none in its range of books on royalty.

✕ Richoux

172 Piccadilly, W1
Tube: Green Park, Piccadilly Circus
Telephone: 020 7493 2204

There are four of these elderly teashops in London. They have a charming décor and serve very good sandwiches and light meals all day, including breakfast. **££**

✕ Wheelers

12a Duke of York Street, SW1
Tube: Piccadilly Circus
Telephone: 020 7930 2460

Wheelers is located on a little street that runs perpendicular to Piccadilly just behind Hatchards. This is a favourite place for us because of the architectural charm. Food critic A.A. Gill described it perfectly: 'With three dining rooms, one on top of the other, it's like eating in a neat train crash.' Marco Pierre White has taken it over and redecorated it in the original leather, brass and wood to keep it true to its roots. Fish is the speciality and tradition is the rule. **££££**

Foyles

www.foyles.co.uk
113–119 Charing Cross Road, WC2
Tube: Tottenham Court Road
Telephone: 020 7437 5660
Hours: 9.30am–8pm Mondays–Saturdays; 12 noon–6pm
Sundays

Charing Cross Road is a book-lover's heaven. You can spend a lot of time roaming this literary neighbourhood of books new, used and specialized. But before you get too involved, make your first stop Foyles, London's most famously huge bookshop.

It claims to be the largest bookshop in the world, and the number of books here is amazing. It isn't terribly organized, but if you love books this is the place for you.

EATING IN FOYLES

Ray's Jazz Café is the newest addition to Foyles. Here, you can enjoy light meals and sandwiches while listening to and shopping for classical jazz or blues CDs and records. **£–££**

✕ Stockpot

18 Old Compton Street, W1
Tube: Tottenham Court Road,
Leicester Square
Telephone: 020 7287 1066

This is always busy because it gives you huge portions and is excellent value for your money. It has lots of choices, serves wine and beer and has a loyal following. The seating is somewhat cramped, but the artwork of Tatler caricatures of Victorian personalities are rather charming. Plus the service is fast. **£–££**

✕ Ed's Easy Diner

12 Moor Street, W1
Tube: Tottenham Court Road,
Leicester Square
Telephone: 020 7439 1955

Sitting on the 'V' of Old Compton Street, across from the Stockpot, Ed's serves American diner food – burgers, shakes and so on. It is very popular and the food is good. **££**

✕ Amato Café

14 Old Compton Street, W1
Tube: Tottenham Court Road,
Leicester Square
Telephone: 020 7734 5733

The sign outside says 'Caffé Pasticceria, Sala da Thé', and the pastries are wonderful. Try the Malaga gâteau, which is really just a pile of chocolate and coffee mousse. **£–££**

✕ Café Bohème

www.cafeboheme.co.uk
13–17 Old Compton Street, W1
Tube: Tottenham Court Road,
Leicester Square
Telephone: 020 7734 0623

This café is just across the street from the Prince Edward theatre (see page 133) and they serve a good-value pre-theatre menu up to 7pm. The

menu is mainly French, but pasta is also available.
££–£££

✕ Maison Bertaux
28 Greek Street, W1
Telephone: 020 7437 6007
Tube: Tottenham Court Road

This little café has been on the same spot since 1871. The neighbourhood has changed and customers have come and gone, but the pastries and croissants remain consistently wonderful. They have never tried to keep up with anyone else, and their menu today is still limited to quiche, sandwiches, Dijon slices, tarts, croissants and the famous pastries. You can get tea, coffee and latte, but none of the fancier coffees so popular at other cafés. The charming lady in charge, Michele, has been here since 1981 and waitress Madame Micallef has been serving 'for ever'. It seems that almost everyone who comes in is greeted by name. **£**

Harrods
www.harrods.com
87–135 Brompton Road, SW1
Tube: Knightsbridge
Telephone: 020 7730 1234
Hours: 10am–7pm Monday–Saturday

This is the most amazing department store in the world with floor after floor of wonders. Make it a destination if you can, and try to arrive near opening time because the crowds become dense as the day wears on. Should you arrive before opening time, take a walk around the building to view all the creative window displays; they will give you a hint of what treasures await you inside. Once inside, head first to the food halls because, when it is relatively quiet, you can see the inlaid tiles and architecture as well as the beautiful displays of food so much better. After that, take the escalators up and browse each floor at your leisure.

Following the huge July sale, the Christmas shop opens (it is next to the book department) and it is dazzling. Strange as it sounds, people are buying ornaments in August with great enthusiasm (me, too). One other detail you should know –

several years ago the management decided to make a charge for the use of the toilets. Despite rage that continues to this day, they kept to this decision and hired women and men to 'guard' the entrances to ensure payment. Noting that customers holding charge cards do not have to pay, I promptly opened an account and shamelessly lend my card to others. So, we now warn, 'It costs a pound to pee at Harrods.'

Since the store is so enormous, if you are with others arrange a meeting point should you get separated. You should also know that although Harrods is terribly elegant and up-market, they do not exploit you on prices. They have, of course, extravagant treasures with astronomical price tags, but for other items such as appliances or glassware and china, they are the same as elsewhere and sometimes cheaper. Please note that Harrods has a dress code of sorts and brief clothing or grungy attire will prevent you from entering the store. There are guards at every entrance to enforce this.

Three streets over is Beauchamp Place, with boutiques, restaurants and speciality shops that are fun to browse.

The façade and multiple awnings of Harrods are now world famous

✕ EATING IN HARRODS

There are 22 places to stop for refreshments throughout the store and all are good, just somewhat expensive. Expect to pay more than you would in a café outside the store. All have menus to peruse so you can read before deciding, but you can choose from bagels to sushi, pizza to cream teas, crêpes to diner food from the cafés and counters, or even go up-market and dine in the more exclusive restaurants. **£–££££**

✕ Patisserie Valerie

www.patisserie-valerie.co.uk
215 Brompton Road, SW3
Tube: Knightsbridge
Telephone: 020 7283 9971

This ever-popular patisserie is as famous in London as Harrods itself, and serves superlative cakes and pastries. See page 140. **££**

✖ San Lorenzo

22 Beauchamp Place, SW3
Tube: Knightsbridge
Telephone: 020 7584 1074

This restaurant was made famous by the patronage of Princess Diana and remains popular with celebrity and other high-profile clients. The cuisine is regional Italian. It can be difficult to get a table. No credit cards.
££££

Harvey Nichols

www.harveynichols.com
109–125 Knightsbridge, SW1X
Tube: Knightsbridge
Telephone: 020 7235 5000
Hours: 10am–7pm Monday, Tuesday, Saturday;
10am–8pm Wednesday–Friday; 12 noon–6pm Sunday

If you are looking for high fashion and cutting-edge trends, 'Harvey Nicks' is the place to go. Extremely popular with fashionable people of every age, you can find the very latest as well as the classics, plus all the big fashion names, in this wonderful shopping emporium. Their newly refurbished Fifth Floor Restaurant is exceedingly popular with those who like to see and be seen and it is always crowded. This is a store that is fun to wander through, and the interesting food and gift area is superb.

✖ EATING IN HARVEY NICHOLS

The **Fifth Floor Restaurant, Bar and Café** is a very smart, slick eatery and a prime destination for many of the up-market shoppers who frequent this department store. The good food is secondary to the fun of eyeballing the 'smart set' dining here. Some feel it is too smoky, but everyone agrees the food is terrific. To book, call 020 7823 1839. Set meals in the evening can be reasonable value.
£££–££££. At the bar, coffee and teas are served along with sandwiches, quiche and salad, sweets and cakes. **££**

The **Yo! Sushi** bar offers a huge selection of sushi and sashimi and is counter service. **££**

Wagamama offers many good noodle dishes and has table seating. **££**

✕ Drones

1-3 Pont Street, SW1X
Tube: Knightsbridge
Telephone: 020 7259 6166

Walk down Sloane Street, away from Harvey Nichols, towards Sloane Square. You will pass a lovely green square and more fashionable shops. Here you will also find Drones. We often came here in the 1970s, but it went into decline and we didn't return for some time. Now, however, Marco Pierre White has brought it back to life with a top-notch menu. Dining here is expensive, but they do serve a less costly set-price Sunday lunch. **£££–££££**

✕ Rib Room and Oyster Bar

www.carltontower.com
Carlton Tower Hotel,
Cadogan Place, SW1
Tube: Knightsbridge, Sloane Square
Telephone: 020 7235 1234

Sometimes nothing will do but a hearty slab of Angus roast beef, especially when it is accompanied by Yorkshire pudding. Although the Rib Room is expensive, the food is terrific. The open kitchen brings warmth to the dining room. The Oyster Bar, which serves lighter meals, is another attraction. Fish and poultry are also on the menu. Not the traditional clubby ambience of Simpson's (see page 16), but just as delicious. **£££–££££.**

The hotel is located midway between Sloane Square and Brompton Road.

Sloane Square and the King's Road
Tube: Sloane Square (then buses up the King's Road)

Sloane Square is at the bottom of the King's Road, which is a good shopping area with scores of boutiques, cafés, interior design shops, home furnishings, clothing chains and much much more. Remember the 1960s fashions, and then the punk look of the 1970s? Well, the King's Road (and Carnaby Street) is where it all started and is now a focus for fashion nostalgia. It's fun to walk up one side of the street then back the other. Peter Jones and General Trading Company are across the (side) street from one another at Sloane Square. But it is definitely worth venturing further if you are a shopaholic.

■ GENERAL TRADING COMPANY

www.general-trading.co.uk
Sloane Square SW1
Tube: Sloane Square
Telephone: 020 7730 0411
Hours: 10am–6pm
Monday–Tuesday; 10am–7pm
Wednesday; 10am–6.30pm
Thursday–Saturday

This is an interesting, eclectic store, popular with Sloane Rangers (wealthy young ladies of the area) as a bridal registry, most notably by the late Princess of Wales. There are many creative, unusual and irresistible things here. The clothing line is limited to pretty accessories; their main attractions are decorative things for the home and gift and garden items. The **in-store café (£££)** offers stylish lunching or just a dessert and coffee. Wines and spirits are available.

■ PETER JONES

www.johnlewis.com
Sloane Square, SW1
Tube: Sloane Square
Telephone: 020 7730 3434
Hours: 9.30am–7pm
Monday–Saturday

This is the sister store to John Lewis on Oxford Street (see page 110). Peter Jones was founded in 1877, was rebuilt in 1936 and has recently been refurbished. It is really a mini-version of John Lewis, offering the same excellent, old-fashioned service, if not as wide a selection of goods.

✕ EATING IN PETER JONES

The upstairs **restaurant** overlooking Sloane Square makes this a good stop. Lovely lunches can be had, and the service is very friendly. Be sure to ask for a window table so you can both people watch and window shop as you feed yourself up in readiness for the long walk of shops that is the King's Road. **££**

✕ Chelsea Kitchen

98 King's Road, SW3
Tube: Sloane Square
Telephone: 020 7589 1330

A couple of blocks walk along King's Road from Sloane Square is this café with a large menu, quick service and low prices (including house wine). If you need fuel for shopping, this is a good choice at budget prices. Open seven days a week. No credit cards. **£–££**

✂ My Old Dutch

221 King's Road, SW3
Tube: Sloane Square
Telephone: 020 7376 5650

Just beyond Manresa Road/Glebe Place (same street, just different names on either side), you can find really good savoury and sweet pancakes (Dutch pancakes are thicker than French crêpes and are enormous) and hearty salads. Seasonally imported Dutch beers are also served. **£–££**

✂ Bluebird

www.conran.com
350 King's Road
Tube: Sloane Square
Telephone: 020 7559 1000

Terence Conran is famous for his restaurants, and this is one of the less expensive ones. They have set price lunches and pre-theatre dinners (until 7pm). The dining room can seat 240 people, and a small army of cooks prepares European and Australian-inspired dishes. Downstairs is a deluxe food market, fun to browse before or after your meal. **££–££££**

✂ Chutney Mary's

535 King's Road
Tube: Sloane Square
Telephone: 020 7836 5314

This is Indian food, among the best you will ever get in London or elsewhere. It is a long way from Sloane Square tube but, if you make it on foot, it will be your reward after all that hard shopping along the King's Road. And you can always treat yourself to a taxi or bus ride back to the tube station afterwards. It is especially nice to dine in the atrium greenhouse with its abundance of palm trees and greenery. Prices are generally in the high to moderate range but always cheaper at lunchtime. Sunday brunch is a fixed price. **£££**

TAKING TEA

The genteel custom of afternoon teatime inspires visions of fine china, dainty sandwiches, scones with jam and clotted cream and lilting background music. And so it is. Don't miss this wonderful ritual that is quintessentially English.

The Georgian Restaurant in Harrods, Knightsbridge is a popular venue for taking tea.

Taking Tea

What could be nicer than tea and scones (and more) in a fancy hotel, small café or any place in between? Below are some of the best places for this wonderful ritual, where you can wear the suit or dress you packed 'just in case' and get out of the jeans and walking-shoe uniform. Of course, should you be out and about and it's teatime and a little café just happens to beckon, by all means enter and enjoy. But for the elegant Ritz and the like you will be glad you took the effort to spruce up (ties and jackets for men, please).

Tea times are from 3pm until 5.30–6pm (last orders). There are several ways to enjoy the tea ceremony so select the one that most appeals to you and your schedule. At the top is the traditional high tea, which includes savouries such as Welsh rarebit, smoked salmon sandwiches, potted shrimps on toast and other tasty morsels followed by tiny pastries, scones, strawberry preserves and clotted cream, biscuits and something chocolatey. Of course, there will be an array of teas to choose from. In season, fresh strawberries and cream will be added to the tray. Less sumptuous is the tea consisting of scones, strawberry jam and clotted cream, along with another choice of sliced layer cake (perhaps fruitcake) and your choice of teas. This choice offers you a rest stop plus a strong infusion of sugar to energize you for more sightseeing (and saves some of your appetite for dinner later on in the day).

TEA AT THE RITZ, FORTNUM AND MASON AND HARRODS

Let's begin at the top with the most famous of all, The Ritz.

The Ritz
www.theritzlondon.com
150 Piccadilly, W1
Tube: Green Park
Telephone: 020 7493 8181

Consider tea at The Ritz as an occasion, and perhaps one of the highlights of your trip to London. You must book well in advance (some make their booking before leaving home), and expect to have an expensive time. However, it is a reasonable price to pay for the grandeur and elegance, not to mention the wonderful array of treats presented on tiered silver trays. Although terribly fancy, it is not intimidating, so just relax and have a wonderful time. Even if you begin your tea as early as 3pm you still won't have an appetite for dinner at a later hour. **££££**

☕ Fortnum and Mason

www.fortnumandmason.com
181 Piccadilly Road, W1
Tube: Piccadilly Circus
Telephone: 020 7734 8040

St James's Restaurant and Tea Salon on the fourth floor is done up Edwardian-style in pale green and beige, formal yet inviting. All of the ritual is here, and all entirely in keeping with the reputation of this fine store. Full tea is served Monday to Saturday 3–5pm. **£££**

The Fountain Restaurant on the ground floor has a less formal atmosphere and is the speedier option for those who do not have all afternoon to linger over tea and cakes. But you will nevertheless experience the tradition and fine manners that accompany the ritual. The amount of food offered is generous – enough to be a pre-theatre supper for most diners. Full tea is served Monday to Saturday 3–6pm. **££–£££**

☕ Harrods

www.harrods.com
87–135 Brompton Road, SW1
Tube: Knightsbridge
Telephone: 020 7730 1234

The Georgian Restaurant is very large and hordes of people come to tea here, but you are still treated well and the silver is in abundance. However, your offerings will not be any better than at less expensive venues. Full tea available with champagne Monday–Saturday 3.30–5.15pm (last orders). **£££**

☕ OTHER TEATIME OPTIONS

All major hotels offer afternoon teas and the ones listed below are among the best. They are open approximately 3–6pm and have a dress code. (Generally **£££**) I've also included my favourite, more modest teatime venue.

☕ Brown's

www.brownshotel.com
33–34 Albemarle Street, W1
Tube: Green Park
Telephone: 020 7493 6020

Reservations are necessary throughout the week, but on the weekends tea is served on a first come, first served basis. Famous for their Victorian sponge cake.

☕ Claridge's

www.the-savoy-group.com/claridges
Brook Street, Mayfair, W1
Tube: Bond Street
Telephone: 020 7629 8860

Art Deco sophistication is the setting, and the treats are top-notch. Book in advance so you don't miss this.

☕ Dorchester

www.dorchesterhotel.com
54 Park Lane, W1
Tube: Hyde Park Corner
Telephone: 020 7629 8888

Dress up in order to feel at home seated on a silk damask chair, surrounded by marble, mirrors and gilded columns, while you take tea.

☕ Lanesborough

www.lanesborough.com
Hyde Park Corner, SW1
Tube: Hyde Park Corner
Telephone: 020 7259 5599

A rarified atmosphere surrounds you as you sit down among brocades, moiré silk and antiques to take your afternoon tea.

☕ The Savoy

www.the-savoy-group.com/Savoy
The Strand, WC2
Tube: Charing Cross
Telephone: 020 7836 4343

On Sunday a teadance takes visitors back to the 1920s, but for the rest of the week, tea is served in a more tranquil atmosphere.

☕ Waldorf

Aldwych, WC2
Tube: Holborn or Temple
Telephone: 020 7836 2400

On the weekends bring your dancing shoes for the famous teadances that are held in the afternoons.

☕ The Muffin Man

12 Wrights Lane, W8
Tube: High Street Kensington
Telephone: 020 7737 6652

'Modest, old, lace-curtained and lovely' describes my favourite place for tea. You can order the tea service at almost any time as they are less rigid about official hours for serving scones and clotted cream. Just a short walk from High Street Kensington tube station, it's in a pleasant spot, and is even open on Sundays. **£–££**

PRE-THEATRE DINING

You can eat well and without rush at many good restaurants during the pre-theatre hours of 5–7.30pm. Book ahead to avoid disappointment, and when considering whether to have a dessert keep in mind that ice cream is sold during theatre intervals. An A–Z of theatres and the convenient eating places for each one is followed by more details on the restaurants.

The Lyceum Theatre, situated near Covent Garden, is surrounded by restaurants, many of which offer pre-theatre dinners.

The Theatres

Adelphi
Strand, WC2
Tube: Charing Cross
Telephone: 020 7344 0055

Maggiore's, Porters

Albery
www.theambassadors.com
St Martin's Lane, WC2
Tube: Leicester Square
Telephone: 020 7369 1740

Café in the Crypt, Mon Plaisir

Aldwych
www.theambassadors.com
Aldwych, WC2
Tube: Temple, Holborn
Telephone: 0870 400 0805

Christopher's

Apollo
29 Shaftesbury Avenue, W1
Tube: Piccadilly Circus
Telephone: 020 7494 5399

Golden Dragon, Kettners

Apollo Victoria
17 Wilton Road, SW1
Tube: Victoria
Telephone: 0870 400 0651

Noodle Noodle, Tiles

Cambridge
www.stoll-moss.com
Earlham Street, Seven Dials, WC2
Tube: Covent Garden
Telephone: 020 7494 5399

The Ivy, Mon Plaisir

Comedy
www.theambassadors.com
Panton Street, SW1
Tube: Piccadilly Circus
Telephone: 020 7369 1731

Le Piaf, Pizza Express,
Stockpot

Criterion
Piccadilly Circus, W1
Tube: Piccadilly Circus
Telephone: 020 7413 1437

Le Piaf, Pizza Express,
Stockpot

Dominion
Tottenham Court Road, W1
Tube: Tottenham Court Road
Telephone: 0870 606 3400

Hugo's Pizzeria and
Rotisserie Bar, All Bar One

🦋 Donmar Warehouse

www.theambassadors.com
41 Earlham Street, WC2
Tube: Covent Garden
Telephone: 020 7369 1732

Mon Plaisir

🦋 Duchess

www.stoll-moss.com
Catherine Street, WC2
Tube: Covent Garden
Telephone: 020 7494 5399

Maggiore's, Porters

🦋 Duke of York's

www.theambassadors.com
St Martin's Lane, WC2
Tube: Leicester Square
Telephone: 020 7369 1791

Café in the Crypt

🦋 Garrick

www.stoll-moss.com
Charing Cross Road, WC2
Tube: Leicester Square
Telephone: 020 7494 5399

Café in the Crypt

🦋 Gielgud

www.stoll-moss.com
Shaftesbury Avenue, W1
Tube: Piccadilly Circus
Telephone: 020 7494 5399

Golden Dragon, Kettners

🦋 Her Majesty's

www.stoll-moss.com
Haymarket, SW1
Tube: Piccadilly Circus
Telephone: 020 7494 5399

Le Piaf, Pizza Express,
Stockpot

🦋 London Coliseum

www.eno.org
St Martin's Lane, WC2
Tube: Leicester Square
Telephone: 020 7632 8300

Café in the Crypt

🦋 London Palladium

www.stoll-moss.com
Argyll Street, W1
Tube: Oxford Circus
Telephone: 020 7494 5399

Carluccio's Caffé, Caffé Uno,
Café Libre

🦋 Lyceum

Wellington Street, WC2
Tube: Charing Cross, Covent Garden
Telephone: 0870 243 9000

Maggiore's, Porters

🍴 Lyric

www.stoll-moss.com
Shaftesbury Avenue, W1
Tube: Piccadilly Circus
Telephone: 020 7494 5399

Golden Dragon, Kettners

🍴 New Ambassador's

www.theambassadors.com
West Street, WC2
Tube: Leicester Square
Telephone: 020 7494 5399

The Ivy, Mon Plaisir

🍴 Palace

www.stoll-moss.com
Cambridge Circus, Shaftesbury
Avenue, W1
Tube: Leicester Square
Telephone: 020 7494 5399

The Ivy, Mon Plaisir, Kettners

🍴 Phoenix

www.theambassadors.com
Charing Cross Road, WC2
Tube: Leicester Square
Telephone: 020 7369 1733

Maison Bertaux, The Ivy,
Kettners, Stockpot, Ed's Easy
Diner, Café Bohème

🍴 Piccadilly

www.theambassadors.com
Denman Street, W1
Tube: Piccadilly Circus
Telephone: 020 7369 1744

Golden Dragon

🍴 Prince Edward

www.delfont-mackintosh.com
30 Old Compton Street, W1
Tube: Leicester Square
Telephone: 020 7447 5400

Maison Bertaux, The Ivy,
Kettners, Stockpot, Ed's Easy
Diner, Café Bohème,
Patisserie Valerie

🍴 Prince of Wales

www.delfont-mackintosh.com
31 Coventry Street, W1
Tube: Piccadilly Circus
Telephone: 020 7839 5972

Golden Dragon, Le Piaf,
Pizza Express, Stockpot

🍴 Queen's

www.stoll-moss.com
Shaftesbury Avenue, W1
Tube: Piccadilly Circus
Telephone: 020 7494 5399

Golden Dragon, Kettners

St Martin's
West Street, WC2
Tube: Leicester Square
Telephone: 020 7836 1443

The Ivy, Mon Plaisir

Savoy
www.the-savoy-group.com
Strand, WC2
Tube: Charing Cross
Telephone: 020 7836 8888

Maggiore's, Porters

Shaftesbury
210 Shaftesbury Avenue, WC2
Tube: Covent Garden, Holborn,
Tottenham Court Road
Telephone: 0870 906 3798

Franks, Mode, Mon Plaisir

Strand
www.trh.co.uk
Aldwych, WC2
Tube: Covent Garden, Temple
Telephone: 0870 901 3356

Maggiore's, Porters

Theatre Royal Drury Lane
www.stoll-moss.com
Catherine Street, WC2
Tube: Covent Garden
Telephone: 020 7494 5399

Maggiore's, Porters

Theatre Royal Haymarket
www.trh.co.uk
Haymarket, SW1
Tube: Piccadilly Circus
Telephone: 0870 901 3356

Le Piaf, Pizza Express,
Stockpot

Vaudeville
Strand, WC2
Tube: Charing Cross
Telephone: 020 7836 9987

Maggiore's, Porters

Victoria Palace
Victoria Street, SW1
Tube: Victoria
Telephone: 020 7834 1317

Noodle Noodle

Wyndhams
www.theambassadors.com
Charing Cross Road, WC2
Tube: Leicester Square
Telephone: 020 7369 1736

Café in the Crypt, Mon Plaisir

The Restaurants

All Bar One

New Oxford Street, WC1
Tube: Tottenham Court Road

This branch of the popular pub/bar chain is just round the corner from the Dominion Theatre. For more details, see page 139. **££**

Café Bohème

www.cafeboheme.co.uk
13–17 Old Compton Street, W1
Tube: Tottenham Court Road, Leicester Square
Telephone: 020 7734 0623

A pre-theatre supper is available until 7pm. For more details, see page 118. **££–£££**

Café in the Crypt

www.stmartin-in-the-fields.org
St Martin-in-the-Fields Church, Trafalgar Square
Tube: Charing Cross, Leicester Square
Telephone: 020 7839 4342

See page 29. **£–££**

Café Libre

22 Great Marlborough Street, W1
Tube: Oxford Circus
Telephone: 020 7437 4106

See page 112. **£–££**

Caffé Uno

Argyll Street, W1
Tube: Oxford Circus
Telephone: 020 7437 2503

One of a chain, see page 139 for more details. **£–££**

Carluccio's Caffé

www.carluccios.com
8 Market Place, Oxford Circus, W1
Tube: Oxford Circus
Telephone: 020 7636 2228

See page 139. **£–££**

Christopher's

www.christophersgrill.com
18 Wellington Street, WC2
Tube: Covent Garden, Charing Cross
Telephone: 020 7240 4222

Pre-theatre set two-course dinner from 5.30–7.30pm. For more details, see page 47. **££–£££**

Ed's Easy Diner

12 Moor Street, W1
Tube: Tottenham Court Road, Leicester Square
Telephone: 020 7439 1955

A good choice if you've got children with you. For more details, see page 118. **££**

✕ Frank's
52 Neal Street, WC2
Tube: Covent Garden
Telephone: 020 7836 6345

See page 48. **£**

✕ The Golden Dragon
28–29 Gerrard Street, W1
Tube: Leicester Square
Telephone: 020 7734 2763

This is one of the best choices for Chinese food in Chinatown. The large menu ensures you will find exactly what you want, and they are open from late morning until well past the final curtain. **££**

✕ Hugo's Pizzeria and Rotisserie Bar
Bedford Avenue, WC1
Tube: Tottenham Court Road
Telephone: 020 7300 5030

This restaurant serves pizzas and pasta with good value house wine. One side of the restaurant (on Great Russell Street) is more casual and is called the Rotisserie Bar, serving lighter meals at cheaper prices. **££–£££**

✕ The Ivy
1 West Street, WC2
Tube: Leicester Square
Telephone: 020 7836 4751

The Ivy is so famous and patronized by so many celebrities that it can be very difficult to book a table. The Ivy first opened in 1911 and has never lost its strength. It remains fun, unpretentious, energetic and glamorous and has great food. However, the most ordered dish on the menu is the humble shepherd's pie.

An early dinner is available for those who prefer to eat before going to the theatre, but meals are also served until midnight to accommodate the post-theatre crowd. **£££–££££**

✕ Kettners
29 Romilly Street, W1
Tube: Leicester Square
Telephone: 020 7734 6112

Established in 1867 by Napoleon III and his chef, this restaurant has undergone many changes over the years. Pizza Express recently purchased Kettners, but the high standard of Pizza Express coupled with the long history of Kettners should mean good eating for years to come. They are open from 10am until midnight. Pre-theatre supper in the adjacent champagne bar is enjoyable. **££**

✕ Maggiore's
33 King Street, WC2
Tube: Covent Garden, Charing Cross
Telephone: 020 7379 9696

Between 5pm and 7pm you can dine elegantly on the set menu, but you must vacate your table by 7pm. For more details see page 50. **££–£££**

✕ Maison Bertaux
28 Greek Street, W1
Telephone: 020 7437 6007
Tube: Tottenham Court Road

See page 119. **£**

✕ Mode, WC2
57 Endell Street, WC2
Tube: Covent Garden
Telephone: 020 7240 8085

See page 48. **£**

✕ Mon Plaisir
www.monplaisir.co.uk
21 Monmouth Street, WC2
Tube: Covent Garden,
Leicester Square
Telephone: 020 7836 7243

See page 49. **££–£££**

✕ Le Piaf, Pizza Express, Stockpot
Panton Street, SW1
Tube: Piccadilly Circus

These three restaurants just off Haymarket offer good food for pre- and post-theatre meals. Generally open until 11pm. All are good value, with Stockpot being the cheapest. **£–££**

✕ Noodle Noodle
www.noodle-noodle.co.uk
16–18 Buckingham Palace Road, SW1
Tube: Victoria
Telephone: 020 7931 9911

See page 25. **£–££**

✕ Porters English Restaurant
www.porters.uk.com
17 Henrietta Street, WC2
Tube: Covent Garden, Charing Cross
Telephone: 020 7836 6466

See page 51. **££**

✕ Tiles
36 Buckingham Palace Road, SW1
Tube: Victoria
Telephone: 020 7834 7761

See page 26. **£–££**

THE CHAINS

Some are ubiquitous and others are genuinely good places to have a meal. The restaurants listed are good value and attain a reasonably high standard of food and service, with some excelling in their field, such as Carluccio's and Patisserie Valerie. Having a branch of a really good chain restaurant close by is often a good thing.

Chain Restaurants

⚔ All Bar One

www.sixcretail.com

These are wine bars/pubs for over 21s. They are almost always pleasant, but more so in the daytime before the after-work crowd pile in. They are fresh and contemporary in style and are open for lunch and dinner as well as Sunday brunch. The food has flair. **££**

⚔ ASK

The food is Italian and they specialize in pizza (they are Pizza Express's main rival). All the restaurants have a good standard of décor and ambience. They can be found all over London. **££**

⚔ Café Rouge

www.caferouge.co.uk

Francophiles call this a 'French McDonald's'. True, it is not a culinary high but all the restaurants have a pleasant French-style décor and the food is fine, if unremarkable. They are in abundance in London, both central and outlying. **££**

⚔ Café Nero

This is the UK's largest coffee chain, and it has a reputation to match its size. The coffee is excellent, particularly the machiatto and espresso. The baristas are well trained, and there is even a Fair Trade coffee option available. You can also get Italian focaccia, panini and pastries to enjoy with the delicious coffee. **£**

⚔ Caffé Uno

www.caffeuno.com

With an open all day policy and the option of getting everything from a hot sandwich through to a full meal. Caffé Uno is a good emergency option. The food is standard Italian fare. **££**

⚔ Carluccio's Caffé

www.carluccios.com

There are 11 branches in total, five of which can be found in central London. Several have great delis attached. The food is uniformly delicious and you can get everything from coffee and a biscuit through a to a three-course meal. They are open throughout the day and evening, and also for Sunday brunch in some locations. **££**

✕ Chez Gérard

www.chezgerard.co.uk

They claim to do the best steak-frites this side of Paris, but unlike similar establishments in France itself, here you can find good vegetarian options, too. Enjoy the French bistro atmosphere and the fixed-price dinner menu. **£££**

✕ Costa Coffee

www.costa.co.uk

The atmosphere is nice in this ubiquitous chain, and the coffee is among the best in town. The cakes and biscuits are good. **£**

✕ EAT

Consistently fresh food plus some out-of-the-ordinary dishes make this a good and delicious choice. Be sure to try the hot sandwiches, they are extremely tasty and very filling. **£**

✕ Le Piaf

We enjoy the changing menu selections and the open-all-day hours; the food is good, the price is right and the décor is bistro and charming. **££–£££**

✕ Maison Blanc

www.maisonblanc.co.uk

There are 13 branches of this chain, with six in central London. This is the place for wickedly good French pastries, breads and savouries. Flour and specialist ingredients are imported from France for the mouth-wateringly good fare that is both traditional and innovative. **£**

✕ Patisserie Valerie

www.patisserie-valerie.co.uk

There are only six branches, but the food is consistently good and the desserts are dreamy. **££**

✕ Pizza Express

www.pizzaexpress.co.uk

They are always reliable and always good for lunch, dinner or anything in between.

Beyond pizza, a few salads and pasta dishes are on offer. They do a particularly good salad dressing. This enormously popular chain just keeps growing. **££**

✖ Prêt à Manger
www.prêt.com

This 'fast food' chain glorifies the sandwich. The food is prepared daily at each location; they have neither a central production factory nor do they employ mass production techniques. Here, fresh is a given. The choices are wonderful, and include sushi and salads. The cakes are superb. **£**

✖ Soup Opera, Soup Works
www.soupopera.co.uk

Both of these chains offer unusual soups and breads, as well as salads and sandwiches, and the variety is overwhelming. **£–££**

✖ Stockpot

Hearty portions, cheap prices and a bistro atmosphere are what you will find in the five branches of this popular dining spot. Possibly London's best food bargain. **£–££**

✖ Tiger Lil's
www.tigerlils.com

Only 3 branches of this more unusual chain – Islington, Bayswater and Clapham Common. Choosing from the iced display, pile on your plate the meats and vegetables you want to eat, tell the cook your sauce, your garnish preference and if you want noodles added, then watch as they deftly stir fry your order over leaping flames before easing your steaming, made-to-order meal back onto your plate. Rice is waiting for you at your table. There is an eat-as-much-as-you-like policy. Lunch **££**; dinner **£££**

INDEX

AUTHOR'S ACKNOWLEDGEMENTS

I am not a chef. I am not even an accomplished cook. However, I do like to eat well in restaurants and cafés that serve truly good food in a nice (charming, if I am lucky) atmosphere at reasonable prices. As the book was written, it became clear that I would need advice from others who were more knowledgeable about food than I am.

So I thank, with much gratefulness, Norma Ackert, who shared her expertise as a cookbook editor and encouraged the project (and me). Mary Jane Jarvis of 'Andre's French Restaurant' in Las Vegas took me further in her accurate advice over the correct usage of French terms. Patsy Inglet, my favourite English authority, supplied me with some valuable corrections. Zerir Baugh's knowledge of historical London added detail and accuracy to my descriptions of some of the major sights, and Kay Siebold came up with the catchy title one evening during a festive dinner party. Mary Capra, a chef, restaurateur and editor, read the final copy and gave me back red ink, resulting in further and much appreciated corrections and improvements.

Profuse thanks are offered to Jo Hemmings and Kate Michell of New Holland Publishers, whose contribution, support and enthusiasm made this book a reality.

Huge thanks to my daughter Jamie Reeves, who read and re-read the many drafts, always with faithful encouragement and good cheer.

However, my husband Bob has to take the most credit for his unwavering support, and his good humour in researching new places when he might have preferred to go back to our old favourites.

Nancy Copeland Ackerman
Las Vegas, Nevada, USA and London, England, UK

PICTURE ACKNOWLEDGEMENTS

All pictures, including those on the jacket, by David Paterson, except:
Spine: Chris Gascoigne & Lifschutz Davidson
Back cover (right): Laurence Dutton (020 7813 2099)
Page 130: Alberto Arzoz.
All line drawings by Madeleine David.